I0181465

Books by this author:

THE SUNSHINE OF MY LIFE

JACK WEBBER
PHYSICAL MEDIUM
– the back story

by

Denzil Fairbairn

published by

Saturday Night Press Publications
England.
snppbooks@gmail.com
www.snppbooks.com

ISBN 978-1-908421-36-4

Cover design by Ann Harrison of SNPP.
The portrait of Jack Webber is by Christopher Smith of St Ives.
The trumpets are those used by Jack Webber in the 1930s.

Dedication

To my Nan and Grampa without whose
dedication Jack Webber's mediumship
may never have developed
and to my wife, Kay who persuaded me
to write this book.

Acknowledgements

My Special Thanks go to:

Clive Branch, of Ewhurst, Surrey – Custodian of the Apported Egyptian Amulet, for his kind permission in allowing me to photograph this important artefact.

Sean Taylor of South Wales, now in eastern Scotland – for the provision of various historical documents relevant to this book and our mutual interest in genuine physical mediumship.

Christopher M Smith of Carbis Bay, St Ives – for the treasured oil painting of Jack Webber shown on the front cover.

Ann Harrison in Lancashire – My Good Friend and Publisher, without whose help and patience this book may not exist.

Psychic News, The Two Worlds and *Daily Mirror* – For their articles in Harry Edwards' scrap book and in their archives, which have provided much towards the contents of The Back Story to Jack Webber Physical Medium.

CONTENTS

List of Illustrations

INTRODUCTION

Many will be familiar with the wonderful book *The Mediumship of Jack Webbe*r which records the séance work carried out by physical phenomena medium Jack Webber and attested to by many serious investigators and newspaper men during the short period from 14th October 1938 until 9th March 1940 when his work in London was being overseen and promoted by Harry Edwards.

Jack was introduced into the London Spiritualist fraternity on 21st April 1938, when an inaugural London séance took place, in a private home. The séance was amazing, and additional invites were extended for Jack to demonstrate again. He returned to London on 7th May and stayed until 10th during which time two more séances were held.

During one of these early séances Harry Edwards met the ex-miner from South Wales and there began a close friendship. It was soon agreed that Jack's future probably lay in London and at Jack's behest, after a few months, accommodation was found for him and his extended family in the London area.

The next sixteen months were truly momentous in the life of Jack and his promoter Harry Edwards, resulting in the publishing of an excellent book detailing Jack's mediumistic achievements and a 78rpm record, captured by Decca Records, of his guide, *Reuben*, singing two Spiritualist hymns. However, the story does not begin there and neither does it stop there.

Prior to the work carried out with Harry Edwards in London, which is very well documented in Edwards' book, many years had been spent in South Wales developing and honing the Spiritual gifts of Jack Webber.

With the aid of family photos and records, other photographs of Jack Webber's physical phenomena, not previously published, together with financial documents, newspaper cuttings and sundry records collected by Harry Edwards, plus memorabilia relating to aspects of Jack Webber the Medium that have been retrieved (indeed salvaged) from the Harry Edwards Healing Sanctuary, the background story can now be told!

Much of the information on the family and the early development in the following chapters has been taken from the personal memoirs of my grandmother, Nellie Evans, which were written as a letter entitled "Family Saga of Psychic Gifts."

Her letter/memoir does carry on to describe other mediumistic members of her family including her daughter, Joan (my mother) – a trance healer, her daughter, Rose – a clairvoyant, Joan's husband, George Fairbairn (my Father) – a trance healer and a medium for church services, and Rose's husband, John Thompson who was a trance rescue medium—with his services being particularly necessary in the years following the tragedies of World War 2.

Now, eighty years after his sudden passing, here is that story.

Denzil Fairbairn
February 2020

Chapter One

The Beginnings

James (Jim) and Ellen (Nellie) Evans lived in rooms situated in Upper Loughor, a few miles from Swansea, in South Wales, with their five daughters, Rhoda, Winifred, Joan, Beryl and Rose. The rooms they rented belonged to one of Jack Webber's older sisters.

Jim and Nellie were introduced to "contacting the dead" by a couple of friends who had invited them to a party in the late 1920s and, of course, as a common diversion in those days it wasn't unusual for a group of friends to sit around a large table in the hope of getting it to move. Nellie recalls that they were all adults, and they sat with fingers touching as their hands rested lightly upon the tabletop. They all began to feel a little nervous, wondering what was going to happen next. What did happen next was that her husband Jim started making strange noises as if someone was trying to speak through him, and with that the group panicked and agreed to bring the evening to a halt. The group spoke together for a period about what had occurred, but Jim continued to make strange noises, so his father and Nellie decided to take him home. They sat up with him for most of that night until he eventually became normal again.

Later that week during a conversation with a friend, an older lady, the discussion came around to Spiritualism. Nellie had to confess she had only a passing interest in it and knew very little about the subject. On hearing this, the lady invited Nellie and Jim to visit her home. The visit was to bring about a turning point in their lives. This friend introduced them to her two daughters and their husbands, and after explaining much about the subject of Spiritualism, they suggested that it would be a good idea for them all to sit around their table. However, recalling what happened to Jim during their previous experience Nellie and Jim were naturally unsure. Their friend continued to try and convince them that all would be well, as they were all quite experienced in these matters. Reassuring Nellie and Jim that they were among people who understood these things, they all took their places around the heavy dining table. They placed their hands lightly on the table top and the same thing happened to Jim as before. Later, they left for home but only after promising that they would visit again the following week, as their friend had said she thought it would be appropriate for them all to start a development circle for themselves.

Jim and Nellie had two daughters in their mid-teens who thought, out of curiosity, they might also like to join the development circle. Along with their daughters, Rhoda and Winifred, they began attending the development circle on a regular basis and it wasn't too long before the power began to build up in the circle. Within a short time, whenever the power built fourteen-year-old Winifred became entranced by an North American Indian guide, who along with other helpers were able to manipulate the table and transmit messages by rapping on the table and tapping out letters of the alphabet. This gave them much in the way of evidence.

At this time Rhoda was 'keeping company' with a young man who worked in the mines and was a member of the Salvation Army. For them to be able to spend more time in each other's company he asked if he could join them on circle nights. He didn't appear to show a great deal of interest in the 'goings on' and invariably he would fall asleep shortly after the start of the circle. Jack's interest was stirred one evening when he managed to stay awake, and thought it would be fun to move the table, but it responded of its own accord. It spelled out evidential information relating to him and caused him to change his attitude to all that was going on. According to Harry Edwards, the information related to a lost handbag containing money, which was successfully found.

After approximately twenty months of development Jack was taken control of by Spirit entities and so began his remarkable journey.

Jack and Rhoda were married in September 1930.

Jack and Rhoda Webber

Chapter Two

Moving Forward

The development circle in South Wales now continued, with both Winifred and Jack as the mediums. Many tense moments were experienced with the guides trying to establish control of Jack, due to the violent way in which lesser entities tried to manipulate his body. Eventually a modicum of control was achieved and it was then that the more familiar controls, became attached to Jack. Soon they were able to become more prominent and begin the work that was destined to take place.

In the early stages much difficulty was experienced in understanding the controls as they had not learned English and would carry on conversations with each other, through their respective mediums, in their own native tongue. It was only by their repeated actions that the guides were able to make themselves understood at these times.

One evening after retiring to bed something strange happened to Nellie. She was thinking about what the Spirit friends were doing for them, when suddenly the walls appeared to fade away and a light began to build up in the corner of the room, by the ceiling. As she watched, the light expanded and soon a tall lady, dressed completely in black, walked in to the newly appeared room of light, which by now filled the whole room, as if lit by sunlight. The lady smiled at Nellie and gradually the whole scene just seemed to fade away. Although startled, Nellie felt that the lady in black was trying to show her a room that she would see again. As already mentioned, at that time the family all lived together in rented rooms, wishing that they had a house, so that they could have a sanctuary of their own.

One day when Nellie was out with her daughter, Winifred, they happened to walk down a country lane where there were four houses in a row. The end one was empty. They asked at the house next door to it, if the empty house was to let. On being told that it was, they asked for the landlord's details and decided to visit him. Upon arrival in his road they weren't quite sure which house was the landlord's so they stopped an old man who was walking towards them, to ask if he knew which house it was. It transpired he was in fact the landlord of the little house in the lane that they wished to know about. He suggested gladly that they should meet him at the house the following day. Feeling sure the guides were trying to help with their move they met him as arranged.

As he opened the door there was a strong feeling of good Spirit presence within. He showed them into the hallway and they passed through an open door into the next room. This was the room the lady in black had shown Nellie. The landlord asked if they liked the house which they excitedly confirmed, and with that he handed over the keys and wished them a good day. It surely was a good day for them as they now had their own house and more importantly, they had their own séance room. Their friends joined them in their new sanctuary and from that moment on the development of physical phenomena gathered pace, with both Jack and Winifred being developed together.

They began to open the door to their 'little house down the lane' on Sunday evenings for Spiritual Services – with Clairvoyance messages following on straight after the service. Initially the sanctuary doors were left open for people to come and listen, and for them to come in and take part in the services on offer. Folks would indeed come into the room and when it eventually became that there was insufficient room they would sit on the stairs or stand in the hallway so they could join in the evening services and the singing of hymns. Their Welsh harmonising must have created a wonderful sound in that little house.

On Tuesday evenings they continued with the home development circle. They were always willing and ready to help any spirit friends that came through. After a short while Winifred's guides were fully controlling her. Her doorkeeper's name was *Toba*, her healing guide was *Bulzar,* and the guides involved in much of the physical work were called *Red Feather* and *Black Eagle. Tai-Ho* was a learned philosopher from the Ming era, *Topsy*, a little black girl, who caused much fun in the circle and then there was *Lola,* a little Indian girl, who gave clairvoyance. Occasionally an old shepherd would materialize in the circle along with his own reed flute on which he would play hauntingly beautiful tunes for the circle members.

It soon came time for Winifred[1] to leave home, which was a very sad time for the whole of the family, but this departure enabled Jack's mediumship to go forward with its own further stages of development. His guides asked for a cabinet to be erected in the corner of the room, but following lengthy discussions Jack refused, saying he didn't want to be closed in. He wanted everything to be done openly. Therefore, a small table was positioned to his right-hand side on which was placed an aluminium trumpet and some toys. All of these were painted with daubs of luminous paint so that, when the lights were switched off, the rim of the trumpet and outlines of the toys could be seen in the dark room. Before each sitting, they would draw a chalk line on the table around the end of the trumpet, as a check at the end of the sitting, to see if it had moved.

1. See Appendix 1 for more about Winifred

They sat for many weeks and nothing happened. Then, unexpectedly, one night the trumpet rose into the air and tilted upwards. It was a wonderful moment for the circle members and the start of things that were thought never to be possible. The toys also began to move about on their own and some would even be placed into the laps of the sitters. Objects began to be brought into the séance room from other rooms, as well as from far off places. On one occasion the sitters could see that Jack's hands had been raised in the air. They had become luminous, glowing brightly in the dark. He was also enabled by his guides to lift red hot coals off the fire, but there was never any damage to his hands. On retiring to bed at night, Jack's bed clothes would be pulled off the bed by unseen hands and a glass of water kept on his bedside table, along with his lamp and cigarettes, would turn blue or some other colour overnight. Gifts were also apported into the séance room for the sitters, including an Egyptian necklace of scarab beetles and a scarab ring for Rhoda, now his wife.

A Tomahawk, with damp earth still attached to it[2], was presented to Jim Evans, the circle leader, from *Black Cloud,* who was of the Mohawk nation, and Jack's main communicator.

Even Jack received a special gift, presented to him by his door-keeper, *Talgar*. This was a blue gemstone, originally worn in his turban when on the earth plane. All these gifts were brought into the séance room from the burial places of the guides working with Jack.

On many other occasions, roses were brought into the circle, still with the dew on them and placed onto the sitters' laps.

Another control working with Jack was *Reuben,* a Jew in this life, who spent many years in South America as a teacher of English and Music. He had a great love of music and was

---

2. See Chapter Six for more on the apports

noted for his wonderful singing voice. Such was the acceptance of Spiritualism in the pre-war years that in 1939 Decca Records formally agreed to record *Reuben* singing during a specially arranged séance held at their Brixton Road studios. (More of that later.)

Malodar, another of Jack's controls, was an Italian Doctor (not a young Egyptian as indicated in Harry Edwards' book) who had mastered the materialization of oils through the palms of Jack's hands, simply by rubbing them together. Whilst Jack was still living in South Wales, it was not unusual for *Malodar* to take his overshadowed medium down to the local marshes to forage for wild herbs with which he would make remedies for those who called on him for healing.

A young lad called *Paddy,* one of the more active workers within the group, was responsible for much of the phenomena. He also helped to bring through newcomers from the spirit world, who wished to communicate. He was like many of the child guides operating through our mediums today, a little bit cheeky, a little bit humorous, but with a wise head on his shoulders.

There came a time, in 1936/7 when it was realized Jack's development had reached such a stage that he was able to start taking bookings for séances away from home. Having given up his work in the mine, his physical mediumship demonstrations initially took him away to different local towns in South Wales where he would work for Spiritualist Churches and Societies. Séances were also arranged and held at the private homes of certain interested parties.

The home circle continued to sit in the hope that perhaps another medium would be brought forward from within the family, and each week they continued to put aside donations in case of future needs. It transpired that with the money in hand they were eventually able to open a little church in a place called Kingsbridge, near Swansea, where Jack and his guides were able to take the first of the regular services and the home circle was now able to carry on its important work. Difficulties were experienced at first, like many new churches, but soon it was regularly and fully supported. Other mediums were booked to take Jack's place on the rostrum, as he was now starting to take bookings further afield.

By now Jack and Rhoda had two small sons shown here George aged 2 and Denzil aged 4

Chapter Three

1937– Spreading his Wings

Before taking the London spiritualist community by storm in April 1938, Jack Webber had become well known as a Spiritualist Medium in his hometown of Loughor and similarly throughout the Spiritualist Churches and Centres in South Wales. As knowledge of his mediumship spread, his popularity began to grow, and details of his unusual work became reported more regularly within the tabloids and Spiritualist magazines of the time.

The South Wales Spiritualist community had been searching for many years in an endeavour to find a successor to such gifted psychics as Evan John Powell, Will Thomas and Trefor Davies. It was felt that Jack Webber was the one to provide the distinct possibility of this gap being filled.

In February 1937 there was a report by *The Two Worlds* weekly journal detailing a request for Jack to attend the home of Mr Reginald Plummer DCM. of Porthcawl, where a two days' visit was sought, and two highly successful séances were held.

The author of this column in *The Two Worlds*, by the name of 'Pressman', attended both very successful demonstrations and goes on to report that by special request a further séance was held a week later, in which direct voice and other phenomena provided a large company of sitters with convincing evidence of spirit returns.

It was explained how Mr George McCracken, the local Sea Scouts Instructor, first tied Mr Webber in an armchair and how 'Pressman' was asked to examine the knots and certify the medium was securely tied into the chair. After an invocation and some singing, the trumpet floated over to Mrs Lewis, of Bridgend, and this lady entered into a long conversation with deceased members of her family, including her father.

After a short interval, a voice, through the trumpet, gave his name as Tom Sweet, of Bridgend, and he was able to give Mr and Mrs Lewis particulars of his earth life and the circumstances of his transition. He then entrusted the Lewises with a comforting message for his wife, to be delivered by them at his old home.

Then came another voice who claimed to be a friend and was accepted by one of the sitters. He told him that a great weight had been lifted from him. "Well, who are you, please?" asked the sitter. "I am Llew Rees and I was killed outright in the colliery. My body was buried under tons of topping." This was verified as true.

Within a short interval a spirit voice exclaimed, "George, I am glad you are present. I am your Aunt Jane." Mr McCracken and his aunt then went on to hold an animated and intimate conversation containing much evidence. After a few moments the trumpet floated away from George and across the circle saying "There is another one present I must speak to. It is my old and trusted friend, Mrs Graham." There was a sense of reality as two old friends greeted one another with feeling and joy.

Then a voice for the Misses Edna and Millicent Davies, of Aberavon was heard. Their father, mother, brother and a friend of their mother spoke for a long time to them giving clear evidence of their identity. These two young women had lost both parents some seven years previously but have now found them again thanks to the wonderful gift of mediumship and Spiritualism.

This was followed by a remarkable form of phenomena. The medium, still in trance, rose from his chair and walked across the room, with all the ropes remaining secured to his body. He shook hands warmly with Mr Turner and whispered a warning to him of things likely to happen in the séance which could spoil everything. Several of the sitters were sensitives and were judged to be giving way to their spirit controls and were thus sapping the power in the room which might easily bring chaos in the séance. Mr Webber returned to his chair and within less than a minute the guide requested that the lights be put on and the knots examined.

Mr Webber was found to be securely tied to his chair with all the sailor-made knots being completely intact. The lights were once again turned down and some old melody was sung. Mr Webber's coat was taken off his person, but the ropes around him were found to be still unbroken and the jacket was later found to be upon the lap of a sitter several yards distant from the medium.

More direct voice evidence followed, this time Mrs Pyne recognized both the voice and the message. Another spirit gave a warning to Mrs Graham concerning some property and deeds which the recipient explained was both timely, valuable and of course evidential.

The sitters were then startled by a voice which filled the room. "Who are you friend?" was the general request from the members of the circle, "E.W," came the answer. "I want to speak to my medium, Mrs W.J. Hopkin." The trumpet then floated across to the writer of this piece ('Pressman') and a voice spoke saying, "You know me."

He responded, "I am not quite sure." Good natured banter followed, and then the voice freely gave the name Edgar Wallace. He spoke about the script which came through his medium Mrs Hopkin, of Porthcawl, some years previously and which was published weekly in a psychic journal over several months. The writer of this column ('Pressman') was in fact responsible for the publication of that entire work which took place quite some years ago making this communication truly convincing to him.

Next, an Egyptian spirit spoke briefly to Mr Reginald Plummer D.C.M. in a foreign tongue, and also in broken English. They happily communicated with each other to the satisfaction of them both.

The circle was indeed not without its lighter moments. Some of Mr Webber's spirit friends, in humorous vein, kept the circle in roars of laughter with original jokes and clever puns. During the singing of a hymn everyone was charmed with a rich tenor voice which rose above the voices of all the sitters and gave a beautiful rendering to those gathered.

"This is a glorious reality!" exclaimed a voice speaking to a sitter from Aberkenfig, and then followed an intimate conversation between friends discarnate and incarnate in the Welsh language in which the famous Welsh "Hwyl" was much in evidence. (*Hwyl: a stirring feeling of emotional and motivational energy*).

In most cases the voices were quite powerful, but in a few cases, presumably through natural emotion and excitement, a few were faint, though every spirit manifesting was clear and fully recognized.

During the séances they also heard the playing of a mouth organ, the ringing of a bell, the rattling of a tambourine and during one of the sittings one child spirit put a skipping rope into the lap of the columnist. All present were grateful for the evidence provided by this young medium, Jack Webber.

Later that same February a report of a rescue situation, involving the mediumship of Jack Webber reached the pages of *The Two Worlds,* entitled "Helping A Dead Man." It reads:

“Rescue work is being carried on in home circles all over the country and great help is being given to those unfortunate beings who have passed on into the spirit world under distressing circumstances, and who, in many cases, are not aware of the change that has taken place.

A case such as this has been brought to our attention by Mrs T Smith, of Porthcawl, who was present at a circle in the presence of Mr Jack Webber which was held at her cottage for the purpose of investigating the cause of the strange manifestations that had been occurring over a period of several days.

It appears that her son, is naturally mediumistic, having seen and described spirit forms on more than one occasion. One evening he retired to bed but was disturbed in the middle of the night by the bedclothes being forcibly removed. Knowing very little about this type of phenomena he was terrified, and it was some time before he was able to sleep again. This happened to him on several occasions.

It was decided to call in a medium, and Mr Jack Webber was approached. He consented to investigate the matter and a circle was held at the cottage. Voices were soon heard, and one entity, an elderly gentleman, spoke to the medium and told him that the room in which the phenomena was occurring had been his own room. Further investigation revealed that some time back he had been drowned but he wasn’t aware that it had happened to him. During this time the medium was shivering as though suffering from the effects of internal cold. A member of the circle was able to speak Welsh and the remainder of the conversation was carried on in this language.

After a time, the spirit communicator appeared to make contact with others on his side of life, who were

> able to explain the position to him and after a short prayer being offered up by Jack Webber, a promise was extracted from the old man to the effect that the disturbances would now cease. The promise was well kept and from that date forward the cottage remains free of manifestations."

Later that year, Jack Webber was contacted by a local family regarding the whereabouts of their family member, a Mr Morgan. As time drew on from his initial disappearance anxiety for his safety increased and search parties were organized and put into action. Family members and friends were out searching for days but found no trace of the missing man. Time passed and, as there was still no news, it was decided, as a last resort, to approach Jack Webber, to ask his help in solving the mystery. A private sitting for the family was consented to. The medium was soon controlled by his main guide, *Black Cloud*, who informed the family that the old gentleman was indeed dead. He had drowned and that his body would be found in five days' time, at a certain spot on the marsh, near to the River Loughor.

As the séance was held on a Monday, Friday was the day taken to indicate the finding of the body. On that day the body was found exactly as predicted, the gentleman having been drowned as indicated. Many thanks and expressions of gratitude were bestowed upon Mr Webber and his guides for all their help.

Towards the end of 1937 *The Two Worlds* published a further detailed report: "Unusual Phenomena at Nantymoel" which truly shows the wonders that can be achieved with cooperation from our friends in the spirit world.

> "The visit of Mr J. B. Webber, of Loughor, to the above church provided evidence of a very convincing nature, emphasizing man's deathless nature and proving

conclusively that Holy Communion, in a practical sense, is an accomplished fact. Every care was taken to exclude possible fraud, the young medium being secured to his chair very thoroughly.

"Light Out" was the signal for the beginning of eighty minutes of the most ceaseless manifestations, in which exclamations of astonishment, laughter and tears, were intermingled. Lights flashed around the circle, sleigh bells were rung in time with the singing—sometimes high in the room, then low, and moving around the circle. A musical box tinkled, castanets rattled, and a kettle drum was played in an accomplished manner. Ladies' hats from one side of the circle were transported to the opposite side and placed on gentlemen's heads; articles were taken out of sitters' pockets and placed in others. A watch which was attached to a heavy chain and medal/fob was carried across the circle and deftly arranged in another sitter's waistcoat, and a tiepin taken from the tie of one sitter was placed in that of another, each of these sitters being gently pricked in the knees during the process.

At the request of *Black Cloud,* the controlling guide, lights were put on and the ropes were thoroughly examined and found to be intact but the medium's jacket had been removed and lay on the floor, while many items from the cabinet, including a table had been lifted out and were strewn throughout the room.

"Light out" again, and the introduction to the room of a new atmosphere. One after another, friends in spirit sought and found the ones they loved, and through the trumpet gave evidence of their identity, followed by consoling messages and kind words of advice – and for a while Heaven and Earth were blending in complete harmony. After a very moving scene, *Paddy*, a boy control, one of the most active controls of the inner circle and instructor to the spirit people who desire to come through, would provide mirth with his quaint wit, in order to restore balance. A spirit who claimed to be H.F. Wright, the composer of "*Abide with Me,*" sang in a rich baritone voice, filling the room with its resonance, ending with a cheery 'Goodnight to all.' Then followed a silence which was broken by a sitter who exclaimed "Look! The medium is up in the air." When the lights were switched on the armchair was empty, the knots still intact, and the medium sitting on the rostrum which was outside of the circle.

When the séance was ended, envelopes which were sealed beforehand and placed in the cabinet were opened and found to contain messages written in pencil, though the seals were intact. Most important of all, from a point of general interest, a copy-book along with a lead pencil which had been placed in the cabinet by a sitter in the hope of receiving a message from his little girl in spirit, was found to contain the following message: "Daddy, I am happy—Daisy." On another page the following message and autograph: "I live! — Dick Sheppard." This message was only shown to a few persons on the Saturday night when the first séance took place.

At the following séance on Monday night a request was made to *Paddy* by the circle leader as follows: "Paddy, a spirit friend signed his name in the copy book at Saturday's séance. We would like confirmation. Can you get the same friend to oblige us again? If it can be done it will be evidence of great value and public interest." (Care was taken to mention no names). *Paddy* promised to do his best. At the close of the séance, when the copy book was opened, they found not one but two signatures. One was a repetition of the former signature of Dick Sheppard, and the extra one was of

Studdart Kennedy (Woodbine Willie).[1] We are told that both were on intimate terms of friendship when here on earth.

The copybook had been carefully examined before being placed in the cabinet and everything on this side was above suspicion. The result was quite unexpected as no-one had even thought of placing the two individuals together. The editor of *The Two Worlds* was asked to compare the signatures but was unable to 100 percent verify their authenticity."

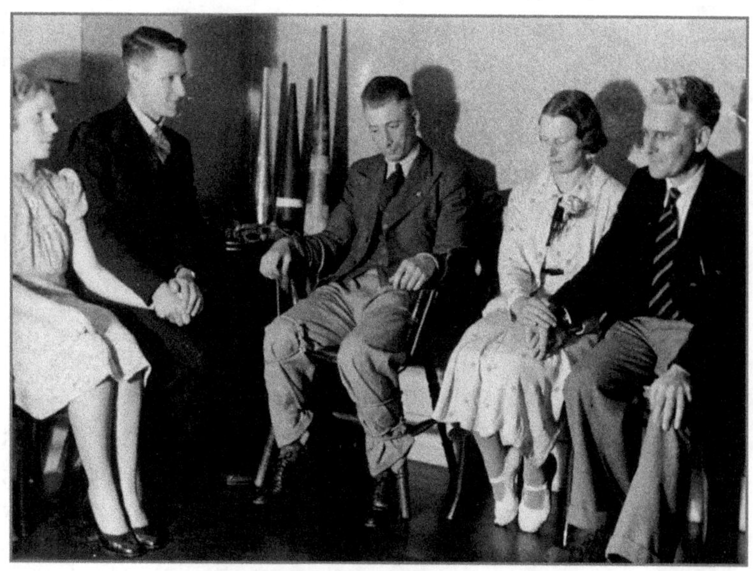

1938 - Waiting for a séance to begin

1. Both gentlemen are sufficiently famous to be found within the listings on Google and it is worth taking a little time to view each of their records.

Chapter Four

1938 – A New Boy in Town

On 19th January 1938, through the courtesy of the Worthing Spiritualist Church, Mrs D. C. Williams writes of the privilege she had of sitting with the direct voice medium Jack Webber. She reports:

> "A cabinet of curtains had been put up at one end of the church annex, the sitters being seated around in the usual way. The medium sat in a wooden armchair outside of the cabinet, to which he was skilfully tied with rope from the back, around his arms and legs; his jacket was fastened with cotton and a piece of tape tied from one wrist, through a buttonhole of his jacket and then securely around his other wrist. Lights were put out and after a fine invocation by the medium's Guide we sang.
>
> Shortly afterward the illuminated tambourine beat time and darted about the room. A skipping rope was used by a child and the sound of small feet could be heard tapping at different speeds. A musical box played, a squeaking rubber doll was manipulated and a small oak table, on which a drum-like tattoo was loudly beaten, danced its way down the room. The most remarkable incident was the removal of the medium's jacket which was flung into my lap. The control then called for a light and this was switched on, the medium being found still firmly lashed to his chair — all knots on inspection were found to be intact, as applied at the start.

Paddy, the trumpet control, amused us with his quaint fun, we were patted and stroked and banged by the trumpet. A powerful voice sang several times and Welsh, Erse (Irish Gaelic) and Hindustani were spoken. Good evidence of identity was given through the trumpet to various sitters, including a pistol shot as a reminder of one spirit's passing. Throughout the séance I was intently watching and listening. Being seated two chairs away from the medium, I was able to hear his heavy breathing throughout, quite distinct from the control's and the other voices manifesting around the room. Towards the close of the séance the control informed us that the medium would be levitated to the ceiling, which was done, with his bumping and breathing being heard overhead. I also heard the scrape of the heavy armchair as he was brought back, the levitation being visible to me.

When the light was switched back on, we found the various articles that had been used—along with the medium's return railway ticket—on the floor at the opposite end of the room, whilst the medium was still entranced and secure in his chair. Lieut. Commander Ford and Mr Allen, who had lashed the medium to his chair, inspected their work and found all the knots intact. Thus, ended one of the most happy, harmonious and evidential séances I have attended in my long experience as a worker. May Mr Webber be greatly blessed in his work for the spirit world. He was an entire stranger to us, but we hope to meet with him again!"

On 2nd February 1938 a voice séance was held at 12 Windsor Place, Cardiff, told here by Mr Harold Brown of Penarth.

"I assisted in roping Mr Webber securely into a chair, and as soon as the sitting commenced a string of beads was placed unwaveringly around my neck. Following the

> manipulation of the tambourine, bell, rattles and skipping rope, a luminous plaque was used to illuminate to me the shadow of a hand with a finger missing. A hand grasped my arm, pulled my ear and then gently pulled my wife's hair. My brother, who passed over ten years ago, and who has spoken to me at previous sittings, gave his name. "Edwin" came the response. I asked if there was anything he wished me to do and he replied "You are doing well. Keep on in your own way and you will achieve much." I asked, "Do you know who is with me?" He replied "I know her very well."
>
> Before the sitting ended the medium in his chair was levitated and bumped across the ceiling before being deposited on the floor about ten feet away from his original position."

Jack's inaugural booking in London took place on 21st April 1938 at the Hendon home of Catharine A. Wilson, Secretary and President of Hendon Spiritualist Fellowship. He had arrived that same day from Wales and the séance was, according to those present, "Amazing." One prominent sitter, who accepted a message, recognized a spirit communicator as a former acquaintance, describing her visitor as 'the last person she expected to speak to that evening!' At Mrs Wilson's invitation, Jack accepted a further two booking dates between May 7th and May 10th for this same London venue.

It was during one of these meetings that Harry Edwards was present as a guest. Contact was formerly initiated between Harry Edwards and Jack Webber. Edwards was so impressed with his mediumship that he began regular travels, accompanied by wife Phyllis, from their London home in Balham, to attend Jack's séances in his home circle. After a while, as their friendship deepened, it became apparent that soon there was to begin the prophesied partnership that would bring to the world the truth of survival into the spirit world.

Before moving to London, several séances were arranged under the auspices of 'The Fellowship of Spiritual Services', at Harry's home. A séance took place around the middle of May 1938 when twenty sitters received remarkable evidence of survival via direct voice.

The medium was securely roped into his chair and a close examination at the close of the sitting revealed that he had not moved and that the ropes had sunk into the flesh, owing to the swelling of his wrists! During the sitting, articles were levitated and rapping noises synchronized with the songs being sung.

The medium's coat was removed and thrown across the room and as soon as this manifestation occurred the lights were turned up to show the medium was still lashed securely in his chair.

A mahogany table, too heavy for one man to lift, was placed near a wall at the beginning of the sitting. This was later found in the centre of the room. The fully materialized heads of various guides were recognized by the respective sitters and the brother of a lady present communicated and gave full details of the tragic circumstances of his passing.

Paddy, a Welsh boy control of the medium, conversed in fluent Welsh[1] with a Welsh sitter, while other communicators spoke freely to the sitters, giving full Christian names and surnames. One spirit voice gave the name "Jack" and asked for "Wilson". A Mrs Wilson was present and after a lengthy conversation with the communicator she revealed that she had visited Jack [*the communicator*] some eight days before. He passed two days later and was buried on the same day that the séance was being held. In this connection an interesting observation was made by the medium's guide, who said that he was able to speak clearly and strongly owing to his still strong connection with the earthly conditions. One gentleman

1. Jack Webber was unable to speak Welsh

spoke to his brother, full names were exchanged, with the communicator remarking "I have travelled a long way from 'The Hill'." This man formerly worked at Ludgate Hill and always referred to his business place as 'The Hill'. To another lady, a brother returned giving the name 'Emlyn' and adding the details of his passing, brought about by an accident with a motorcycle.

Hands materialized, touching a number of those present, while water was generously scattered about the room. The report finished with—"This outstanding demonstration of physical phenomena proves Mr Webber to be one of the most capable physical mediums in the Movement today and the gratitude of all Spiritualists is due to him for the fine work he is doing."

Colin Evans, the allegedly fraudulent medium, had booked to attend a Jack Webber séance during July 1938, organized by and to be held at the home of Mr Leslie Flint, the well-known Direct Voice medium of high standing. However, due to trance and clairvoyant church work commitments of his own, he was late arriving at Mr Flint's home and accordingly was refused entrance to the séance. Fortunately, Mrs Wilson, president of the Hendon Spiritualist Fellowship, also in attendance at Leslie Flint's home that evening, invited Colin Evans to attend at her home the following evening where Jack was booked to demonstrate his mediumship. Colin Evans goes on to say in his report:

> "I had not previously met this medium or had any communication or contact with him except for an informal introduction and an odd word or two casual greetings. During the séance and after a great deal of very impressive physical phenomena and a certain number of direct voice communications for other sitters, which they accepted as evidential, a voice utterly unlike the medium's and which to the best of my carefully critical judgement was exactly

> the voice, in earth-life, of my Father. He addressed me by a Christian name which I now never use, but by which my father always addressed me. A name, moreover, which the voice pronounced in a way in which that name is not usually, nor correctly, pronounced but which was the pronunciation that my father and my family, at home during my childhood, always used! On my not immediately responding, my father (as I am convinced it was) repeated the same name, adding my original surname which I have changed since my father's death. Both these names, Christian and surname, were and are to the best of my knowledge unlikely to be known to the medium or indeed to my host or to anyone associated with either of them. The voice and intonation were those of my father, very individual and very recognizable, who was a university man of literary culture, whereas I do not think the medium Jack Webber will be offended at my mentioning that his own speech and accent are more those of the elementary schools in neighbourhoods mainly populated by manual workers. The few moments of conversation with my father which followed, while not producing any fresh evidence, was thoroughly consistent with his personality."

It was through Harry Edwards' interest in the subject of Life after Death and the Spirit World that he had sought out Jack Webber, in order to make a closer study of the subject. 'The Fellowship of Spiritual Services' (Spiritual Healing and Psychic Development Centre) was begun with Jack Webber demonstrating Physical Phenomena for private groups and Spiritualist Churches and Harry Edwards continuing to provide Spiritual Healing along with the help of Mr J Rosser from his home at 11 Childebert Road. On 23rd July the top advert opposite appeared in *Psychic News* followed by a second one on September 3rd (lower advert).

Healing Services suspended until August 12th.

FELLOWSHIP OF SPIRITUAL SERVICE

11 Childebert Road, (Elmfield Rd.), S.W.17
Streatham 0323 (Harry Edwards).

Spiritual Healing, Mondays, 3 & 8.15 p.m.,
HARRY EDWARDS. J. ROSSER
Absent Healing Arranged

Aug. 30th, 31st, Sept. 2nd and 3rd
JOHN WEBBER.
Physical and Direct Voice Medium.
Write for particulars.

HOUSE OF UNITY

FELLOWSHIP OF SPIRITUAL SERVICE

11 Childebert Road, (Elmfield Rd.), S.W.17
Streatham 0323 (Harry Edwards).

Spiritual Healing, Mondays, 3 & 8.15 p.m.,
HARRY EDWARDS. J. ROSSER
at other times by appointment.

Absent Healing Service.
Tuesdays, 8.30 p.m.,

JOHN WEBBER,
Direct Voice and Physical Medium
Next visit, November 8th, 9th, 10th & 11th

(Printed with permission of Psychic News)

On September 10th *Psychic News* carried the following report:

Reporter Is Addressed By "Dead" Colleague At Voice Sitting

With the headlines, "*Whispering Spirit Gives Nickname of Dead Friend: Reporter Relates Amazing Experiences at Séance,*" the *Balham News*, which circulates in South-West London, graphically described last week a sitting with John Webber, the South Wales physical medium.

"The séance reached its climax when one of the three trumpets hovered in front of the reporter's face, and the nickname of an old friend, who passed on two years ago, was uttered. The voice of this spirit addressed him, saying, "We shall meet again. I am so glad you are interested and have come here tonight."

Seated next to the reporter was a companion, the only other person present who knew the spirit while on earth. The trumpet left the journalist and gave his neighbour a reassuring pat on the shoulder accompanied by a word of greeting.

It took several minutes for two men to rope the medium to a chair prior to this séance, which was held in the home of Harry Edwards, the well-known Balham spiritual healer. Five seconds later the medium's jacket was thrown on to the knees of the reporter! The light was switched on, and the medium was found to be securely tied to his chair!

Transported Medium

While still in his bonds the medium's shoes were removed with laces intact, and Webber was transported out of his chair, returned to his seat and levitated in his chair to the ceiling.

The newspaper man was impressed with what he

called "one of the most striking of the phenomena" – a powerful voice leading the singing through a trumpet. "The voice was of amazing tone," he wrote, "and came through the trumpet at more than 'loud-speaker strength'."

Materialisations seen

After several spirit voices had spoken, including that of a child who was identified by her mother present, there were materialisations.The features of an Arab and a nun were clearly visible as they were built up over a luminous slate.

When the reporter felt a thud and found the medium's coat on his knees, the light revealed that Webber was still secure in his ropes. Yet the interval between the jacket falling in the reporter's lap and the switching on of the light was under five seconds.

"Things happened swiftly," wrote the reporter. "One moment the medium was safe in his chair, and the next he was standing with arms outstretched the other side of the room. The singing stopped abruptly at the amazing scene, but the guide urged us to continue. 'There is not enough power to get him back to the chair,' he said.

Within a minute Mr. Webber was back in his chair, and after a close scrutiny by the men responsible for tying him, they declared that the cords had not moved an inch."

Moving chair

"This was not all, for a sitter next to the medium reported that the chair had gone. From the other side of the circle came the news that two sitters could feel the medium's feet and the chair legs pressed against their faces. In a few moments, at the close of the sitting, the medium was still in his chair about ten feet from his original position at the start."

Spirit Gave His Nickname

Harry Edwards adds: "The spirit who spoke to the journalist gave his name as 'Mo', a nickname for Mowforth. He was a Press reporter who worked on the *Balham News* and passed over two years ago.

As the light was put out for the medium's return to his chair, he was gyrating, suspended just above the floor, and his return to his chair in darkness from a twirling condition provided another example of the amazing powers of *Black Cloud*, his guide.

For a number of minutes, a heavy trumpet was swung about the circle at amazing speed, so that the luminous paint showed as a continuous line. The trumpet came within an inch of the heads of the sitters – another 'impossible' human feat in darkness, or, as the Press reporter said, 'impossible in light'."

Nellie and Jim carried on running the Kingsbridge Church when Jack initially moved away in the second half of 1938, but such were the family ties that it wasn't long before Jack realized that he did not wish to leave them back in Wales. Accommodation was sought, and on Friday 14th October 1938, Jack and his extended family moved away from Wales and into No 13 Childebert Road, Balham, London S.W.17, directly next door to Harry Edwards and his family who resided at No 11 (*see opposite*).

Nellie and Jim believed that the time had come for them to take a back seat in Jack's development work but this turned out not to be the case, as Harry began a new development circle in his own home for a different kind of phenomena. This circle was for infra-red photography and materialization of spirit people. A great deal of success was achieved in both areas – cut short with the untimely passing of the medium just fourteen months later.

Nos. 11 & 13 Childebert Road, Balham

This Book to be handed over to Owner or Agent at the end of each Quarter for Balancing purposes.

RENT BOOK

Tenant's Name Mr J. Webber

Address 13 Childebert Road SW17

Rent £1-10-9 per week in advance

Date of Entry [illegible]

No. 2 C.

HOUSING ACT, 1936

(Sections 58, 59 and 61).

PRESCRIBED FORM OF SUMMARY.

1. After the 1st January 1937 day of .... an occupier who causes or permits his dwelling to be overcrowded is liable to prosecution for an offence under the Housing Act, 1936, and, if convicted, to a fine not exceeding five pounds. Any part of a house which is occupied by a separate family is a "dwelling."

2. A dwelling is overcrowded if the number of persons sleeping in it is more than the "permitted number," or is such that two or more of those persons, being ten years old or over of opposite sexes (not being persons living together as husband and wife), must sleep in the same room.

3. The "permitted number" for the dwelling to which this (Rent Book) ( ) relates is [illegible] persons. In counting the number of persons each child under ten years of age counts as half a person, and a child of less than one year is not counted at all.

4. The Act contains special provisions relating to overcrowding already existing on the above-mentioned date or which is due to a child attaining the age of either one or ten years after that date, or which is due to exceptional circumstances. Full information about these special provisions and all provisions as to overcrowding can be obtained free on application to the Local Authority whose address is [illegible]

Printed and Published by
The Estates Gazette, Ltd., 33, 34 & 35, Kirby Street
London, E.C.1.

Detail of the Rent Book for 13, Childebert Road, Balham

Alongside Edwards' own appointments for Healing sessions and answering hundreds of letters requesting absent healing, the many séance bookings he now put into motion on behalf of Jack's work had to be managed very carefully. The name for the group eventually evolved into the 'Balham Psychic Research Society', with Harry Edwards naturally remaining as its Leader. His knowledge of organizing and provision of literary and book-keeping skills made him the obvious choice for heading the new Society.

Typically, he would post out individual reminders to those attending one of Jack's home circles which would read:

> *Dear Friend,*
>
> *I have pleasure in sending this confirmation/reminder that……… seat(s) have been reserved in your name for the sitting with Mr Jack Webber on………….day, ………………………………1939.* [2]
>
> *The sitting will take place at No 13, at 8-00 p.m. Prompt. Please try to arrive about 7.30 to 7.45. As no one can be admitted after the sitting has commenced.*
>
> *The presence of each sitter implies unconditional acceptance of the séance conditions and will be required to sign an undertaking to this effect.*
>
> *It is requested that the booking fee of 7/6d* [3] *per sitter be sent to me at least one week before the date of the sitting, as otherwise the seat(s) may be offered elsewhere. This procedure has been made necessary owing to people in the past reserving seats and failing to appear, thus thus depriving others of the opportunity to sit.*
>
> *Yours truly,*
>
> HARRY EDWARDS.

---

2. We assume the format would have been the same in 1938 but this is what was inherited with the other papers.
3. 7/6d or 7 shillings and sixpence...equates to around £16.00 today

Those who were to sit would have received these detailed "Séance Conditions":

REQUIREMENTS & OBSERVATIONS FOR A SÉANCE WITH MR JACK WEBBER

Séance Room. *The room must be totally darkened. Artificial white light (not red).Wooden armchair,* ***,*** *with arms, suitable for roping the medium to the chair. Small table on which the medium's articles to be placed.*

It is best to situate the medium in a corner of the room, farthest away from doors and windows. The table to be placed in the corner and the medium's chair next to it. Remainder of chairs around the walls or in a circle.

Special Duties. *A responsible person to act as Chairman to sit next to the medium. A second reliable person to sit next to the table. If the medium does not bring a friend to operate the white light switch, a third reliable sitter for this duty. As a rule, Mr Webber brings a friend with him for this service.*

General Conditions. *The sitters must remain linked throughout the séance. The sitters next to the medium and table to link back, i.e. to hold with both hands the hand of the next sitter. If at any time, for any purpose, a sitter desires to unlink, the sitter should ask the Chairman, who in turn will ask the Guide for permission.*

In any event unforeseen, such as a sitter becoming faint, etc. the Chairman must be informed and who will ask guidance from the Guide. <u>Under no circumstances is any action to be taken until the Guide gives directions</u>.

The séance conditions must not only be signed for by each sitter, but they should again be read out before the entry of the medium. Stress that no object AT ANY TIME is to be touched in any way – <u>also that it is literally true</u>

that the medium's life is in the hands of the sitters and they must guard it well.

If the door cannot be locked a catch is to be provided. Telephone to be disconnected (this can be done beforehand by phoning the Exchange). Singing is required, not only hymns but lively melodies. Singing should be maintained during Phenomena but should not be so hearty that the spirit voices cannot be heard. The Chairman should be on the alert for the voices to hush the singing.

Sitters to whom phenomena, such as materialized hands come should describe to the others what is happening, size of hand and what it does. Remember no harm will come to the sitters (this should be stressed).

If water is felt, it is the de-vapourising of the atmosphere.

The Medium. *The medium should be kept apart from the sitters before the séance. Mr Webber is willing to meet sitters afterwards. As the medium does not take any meals before séance, light refreshments (sandwiches (meat) etc.) and plenty of tea, should be provided.*

If any sitter has any doubt as to the character of the phenomena, the sitter can ask through the Chairman, if the Guide will give explanation or demonstrate the point in question. Psychic rods can at times be seen against illuminated articles.

Then, finally, they had the Covenant which had to be read and signed by each and every sitter attending one of Jack's demonstrations:

CONDITIONS FOR A SÉANCE WITH MR JACK WEBBER (HEREINAFTER CALLED THE MEDIUM) - TO BE HELD ON……………………………….. 1939

I, the undersigned, honourably undertake to faithfully abide by and agree to the following provisions and covenant.

Provisions.

1. No legal process is to be instituted against the medium, his agents or the organisers.

2. No results of any kind are promised or guaranteed.

3. I declare on my honour not to take any torch or light instrument into the séance room or to produce light in any form during the séance.

4. I declare on my honour that I will not touch in any way any trumpet or article used by the medium whether in movement or stationary, in levitation or after levitation.

5. I declare on my honour that I will not touch the medium during the séance or obstruct the phenomena or commit any act of interference of any kind during the séance.

6. To remain linked through the séance.

7. Should I desire to unlink I will first ask the Chairman for permission through the Guide.

8. I agree to obey the Chairman's instructions in all matters.

9. In any case of doubt speak to the Chairman immediately who will ask the Guide for explanation or demonstration of the point in question.

<u>Covenant.</u>

We, the signatories to this agreement jointly and severally covenant to indemnify the medium for any loss or harm occasioned to him by the violation of any of the above provisions and to provide for the maintenance of the medium, his wife, children and dependants in the event of illness or his passing resulting from such violation.

I hereby declare the following to be my true name and address:

NAME...

ADDRESS ....

....

It had obviously become necessary to make clear these points of interference with the phenomena and the introduction of light into the séance rooms, as several reports in the psychic press indicated.

Soon after Jack and his family arrived at 13 Childebert Road, in October 1938 Harry Edwards took the first photos using an infra-red filter, a 800watt photoflood lamp and an exposure of approximately 30 seconds, to see if it was possible to photograph the phenomena.

Now, thanks to the wonders of technology without having to print these in a darkroom, we can show them as "positive" prints as well. The definition is not brilliant but considering these were experimental they show it was definitely possible.

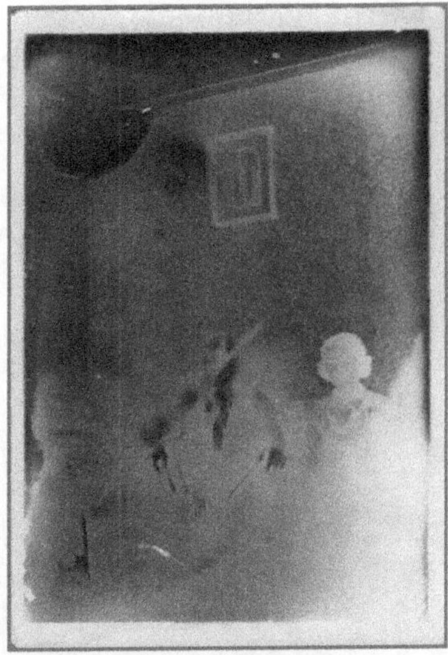

Negatives of the first photos taken in 1938 (from the archive)

Positives of the first photos taken in 1938 (inverted in Photoshop)

Left: Jacket being removed from restrained (roped) medium.
Right: Trumpet airborn in front of medium's face.

Around the same time, under 'The Fellowship of Spiritual Services', Harry Edwards produced the flyer, shown below and on the facing page, to advertise Jack's sittings at Childebert Road.

BLACK CLOUD.
Chief Control of Mr. J. Webber

Inspirational drawing by Harry Edwards

Mr. JACK WEBBER

Mr. Jack Webber, the Welsh physical medium has taken up permanent residence in S.W. London, thus enabling Spiritualists of London and district to witness physical mediumship of a very high order.

His mediumship comprises, levitation, direct voice, materialisations and other forms of physical phenomena (see press extracts overleaf).

No cabinet is used, the medium being roped in a chair in the circle, so that the phenomena is clearly seen by all.

While the sittings are at present held in the dark the light is put on at intervals, immediately before and after phenomena, thus proving the mediumship.

Published testimonies have appeared in the Psychic Press from representives of the "Psychic News," "The Two Worlds," Mr. Harold Sharpe, Mr. Colin Evans and officials of spiritualist organisations.

Those desirous of booking a sitting with Mr. Webber should communicate with the writer at the address below.

Harry Edwards

THE FELLOWSHIP OF SPIRITUAL SERVICE,
11, CHILDEBERT ROAD, BALHAM, S.W.17
Telephone : STReatham 0323

Shortly afterwards, Leon Isaccs was introduced to the circle. He was the photographer for the *Psychic News* as well as other publications and had quality equipment to take infra-red photographs.

Leon Isaacs with the infra-red equipment and cameras

Soon the first "official" photographs of the phenomena were taken by him.

Two of the first photographs of the phenomena taken by Isaacs in early November 1938 were artistically presented to show off the phenomena, by blurring the surroundings.

The first shows a protrusion of ectoplasm, probably an ectoplasmic voice box, close to the medium's throat and from it an ectoplasmic extension to the trumpet – the end of which can just be seen, for the voice to be produced (see opposite).

The second photograph (overleaf) shows two ectoplasmic structures which are supporting two trumpets simultaneously.

Ectoplasmic voice box, in front of the medium's throat and an ectoplasmic extension (tube) to the trumpet. Note the jacket previously removed lying at the medium's feet.

Ectoplasmic structures extend from the medium's mouth and solar plexus to support two trumpets, the ends of which can just be seen.

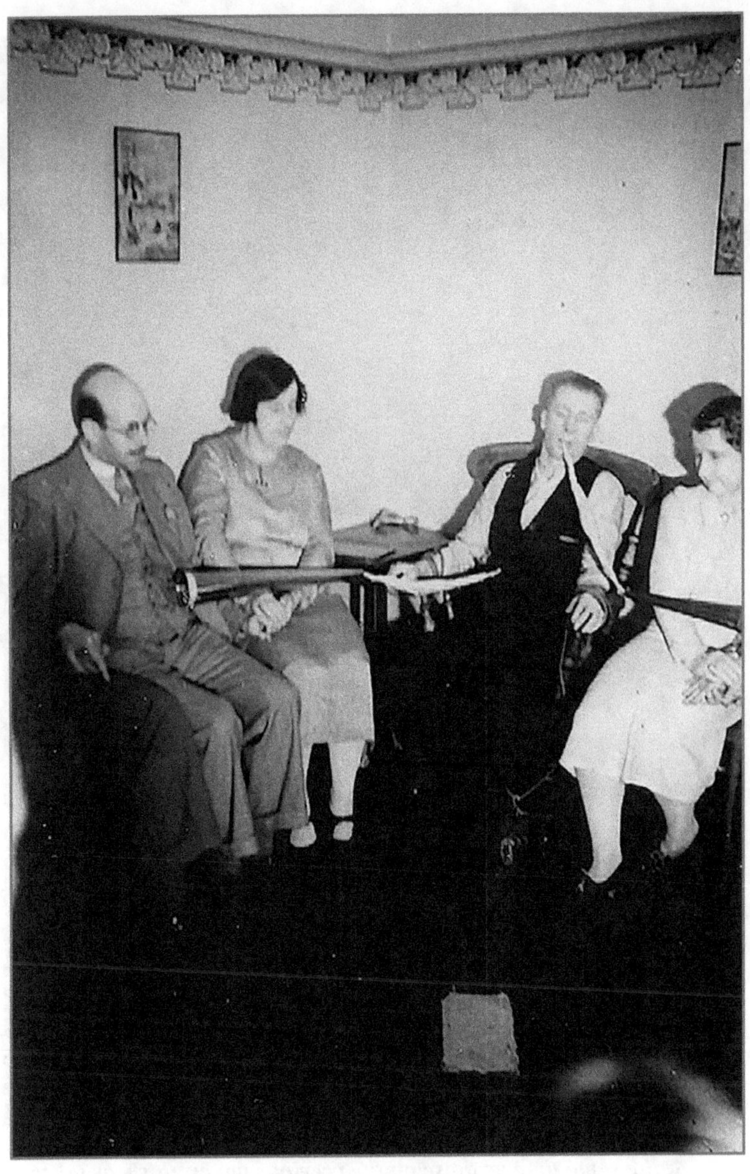

The original of the artistically finished photo on the previous page is identical with this which included some of the sitters.

At the same time as those on the previous pages, this was taken from a different angle.
Jack's wife, Rhoda, is to the right of the picture and her mother, Nellie Evans on the left.

PSYCHIC NEWS

Psychic News

LIFE AFTER DEATH PROVED

THE SPIRITUALIST NEWSPAPER WITH THE WORLD'S LARGEST CIRCULATION
(ON SALE EVERY THURSDAY)

No. 340 — LONDON: NOVEMBER 26, 1938 — Price TWOPENCE
(Registered at the G.P.O. as a Newspaper)

INFRA-RED TAKES YOU BEHIND THE SCENES OF A SEANCE

"*HOW does the trumpet move?*"

Thousands have asked that question when they have heard of how, at a direct-voice seance, the trumpet generally used for the amplification of a spirit voice moves in the air.

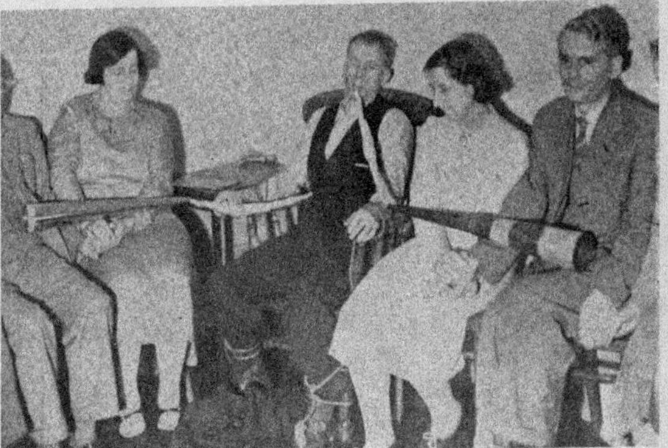

When first the infra-red ray was discovered "Science" said, "Ah, now we shall be able to expose these dark seances!" The reverse has happened—it has proved their genuineness.

Sitters at such seances have often heard a spirit guide explain that most of the power comes from the medium and that it pours forth in the form of ectoplasm which can only build up in darkness.

The guides have also said that the ectoplasm is connected with the medium's body and that it is dangerous to touch the trumpet, unless permission is given, because the ectoplasm, which is a living substance, would rush back to the medium's body and in all probability injure him.

WHAT THE SCEPTICS SAY

"Ah," sceptics have said. "That is how they explain away the darkness and the holding of hands. Actually, they sit in the dark so that fraud can be committed. They are made to hold hands so that they cannot prove that the medium is doing it—to prevent anyone from exposing it."

Well, here is a photograph, taken in London, last week, which proves what the guides say. The infra-red ray has at last made such a picture possible.

BUILDING FROM THE MEDIUM

Jack Webber, the South Wales miner, is seen in trance while two ectoplasmic "rods," one coming from his mouth and the other from his solar plexus—usually from these sources the guides have always said could ectoplasm build up—which are holding the trumpet in the air.

Immediately after the picture was taken these trumpets were whirling round the room with lightning speed.

All the sitters, it will be seen, are holding hands. The medium is tied in the chair, so that he cannot move.

Now, how does "Science" explain this?

Researchers have jeered at ectoplasm. Harry Price, the Goat Man, was allowed to say in a B.B.C. broadcast, the other week, that it was "regurgitated cheesecloth" and "chewed-up dental paste."

All that, of course, is childish nonsense, which he would not dare to repeat in the presence of an experienced Spiritualist.

Just before the photograph was taken, the medium's guide said what the picture would show.

Now it proves what Spiritualists who have studied the direct-voice have always claimed—that the intelligence which controls the phenomena does not belong to any of the sitters or the medium.

It explains the long sittings which usually have to go on before these powers are developed and the medium is ready to be used so that the voices of the "dead" can speak independently.

The power has to be collected, moulded and intensified. In some circles, it has taken years.

In the Hannen Swaffer circle it took three years, although the first voice was heard only a week after Frank Decker, the American medium, had visited the circle and, so said his guide, "left some of his power behind."

You can laugh at the means used by the spirit world. You may call it "clumsy," "tawdry" or "crude." But so is birth, which is much more ugly.

Actually, of course, the "dead" have no material hands, no earthly sense organs of any kind. Their bodies have been left behind in the grave.

Returning to a material world, they have to use material things to make their presence known to us. Otherwise, with our physical eyes and ears, we could not see or hear them.

Ectoplasm, obviously, is a substance which can be moulded by spirit operators. It is semi-physical. It has life, for it can take any form.

Without the permission of the guides, it cannot be touched.

This photograph gives an indication of what has to take place behind the scenes of a seance.

It looks easy enough when, in the dark, you see an illuminated trumpet rise in the air and move rapidly about the room. Actually, months of preparation have to go on before it starts.

Well, whatever you may say, how do you explain away this photograph?

[*This picture was taken for "Psychic News" by Leon Isaacs. It is the copyright of the Fellowship of Spiritual Service, Balham, where the seance was held.*]

On November 26th 1938 'Psychic News' ran this as their Front page story, with a report by Harry Edwards. The photograph is the original of the enlargement on page 52.

(Printed with permission of Psychic News)

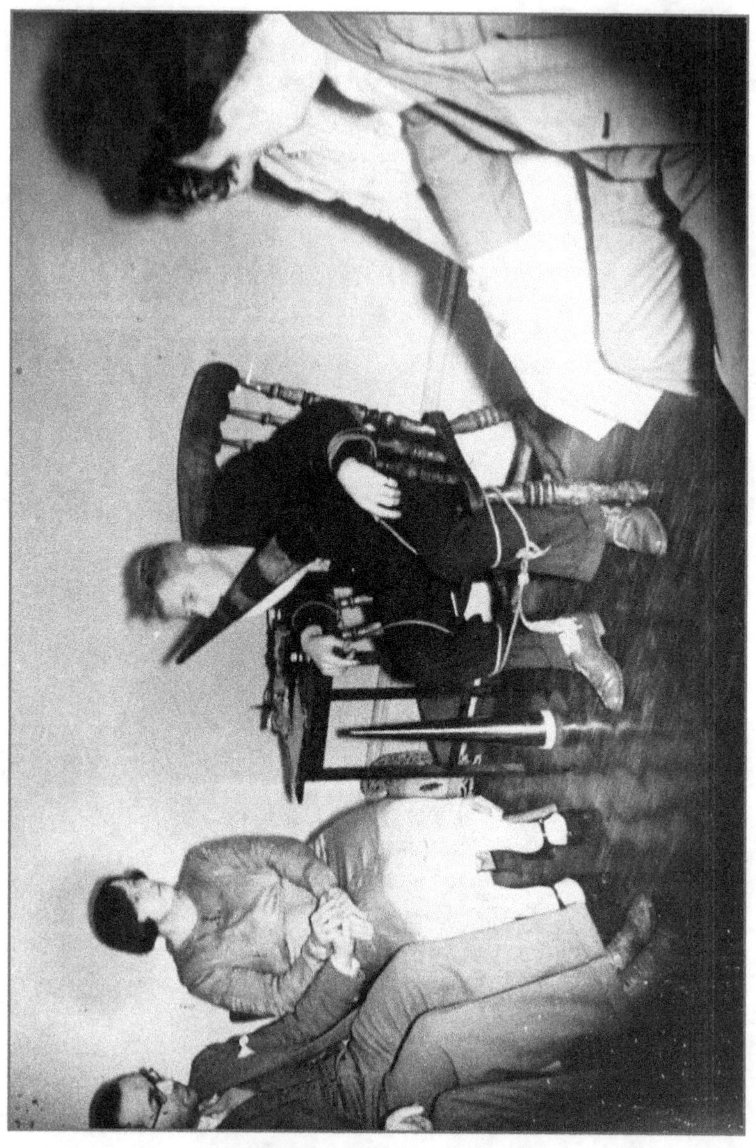

On another occasion this photograph was taken, showing the trumpet being held to the medium's mouth by an ectoplasmic structure from the solar plexus.

The photograph has been rotated to allow maximum enlargement.

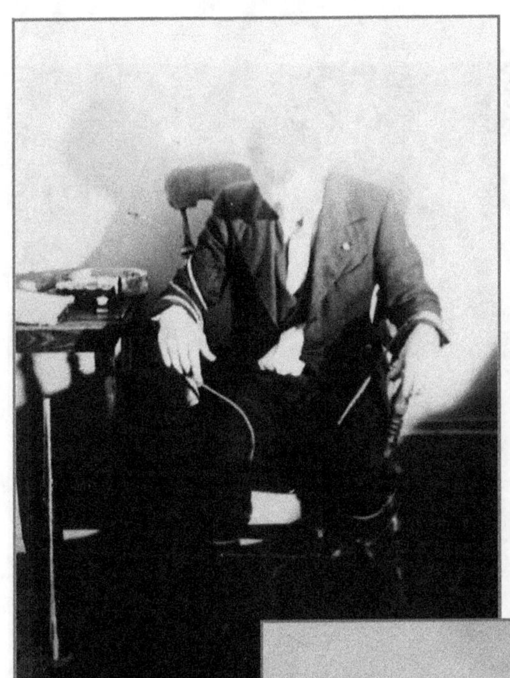

Around the same time Leon Isaacs also took these:

Left: An ectoplasmic extrusion can be seen emanating from the medium's solar plexus area.

Right: An ectoplasmic extrusion can be seen emanating from the medium's solar plexus area to support the trumpet.

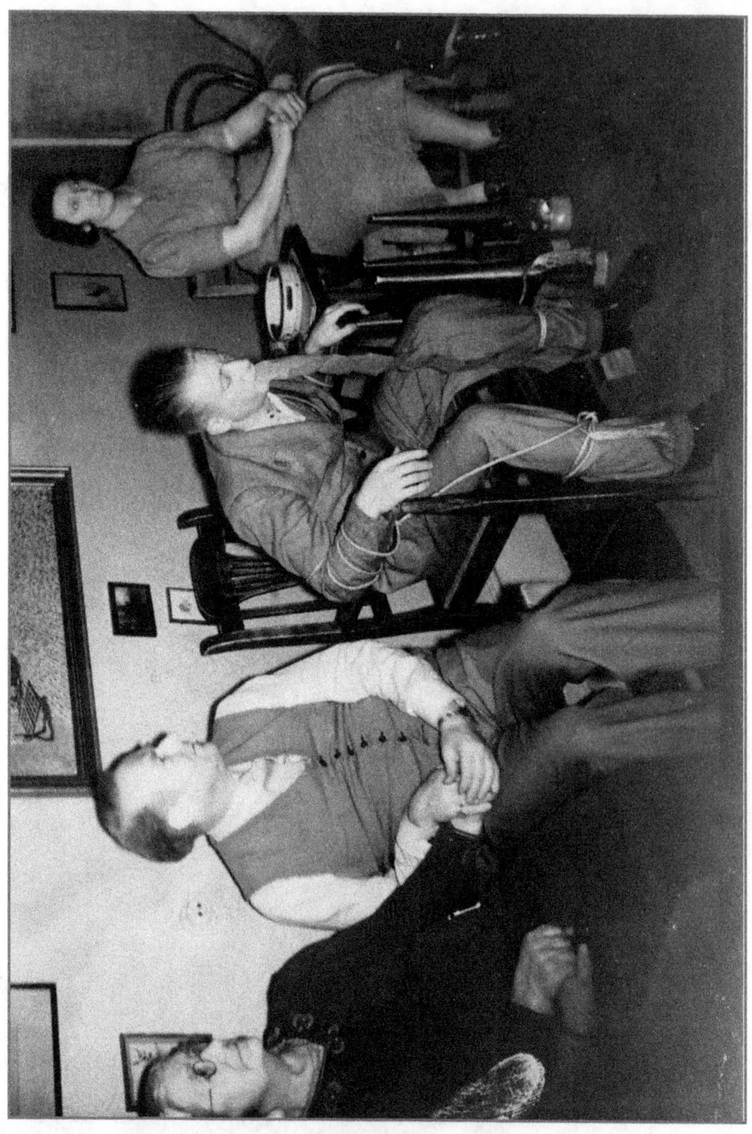

Towards the end of 1938, this photograph, showing zig-zag crinkled ectoplasm flowing from Jack's mouth, was taken by Leon Isaacs at a séance held in the séance room of the medium Harold Sharp (to the left of the picture).

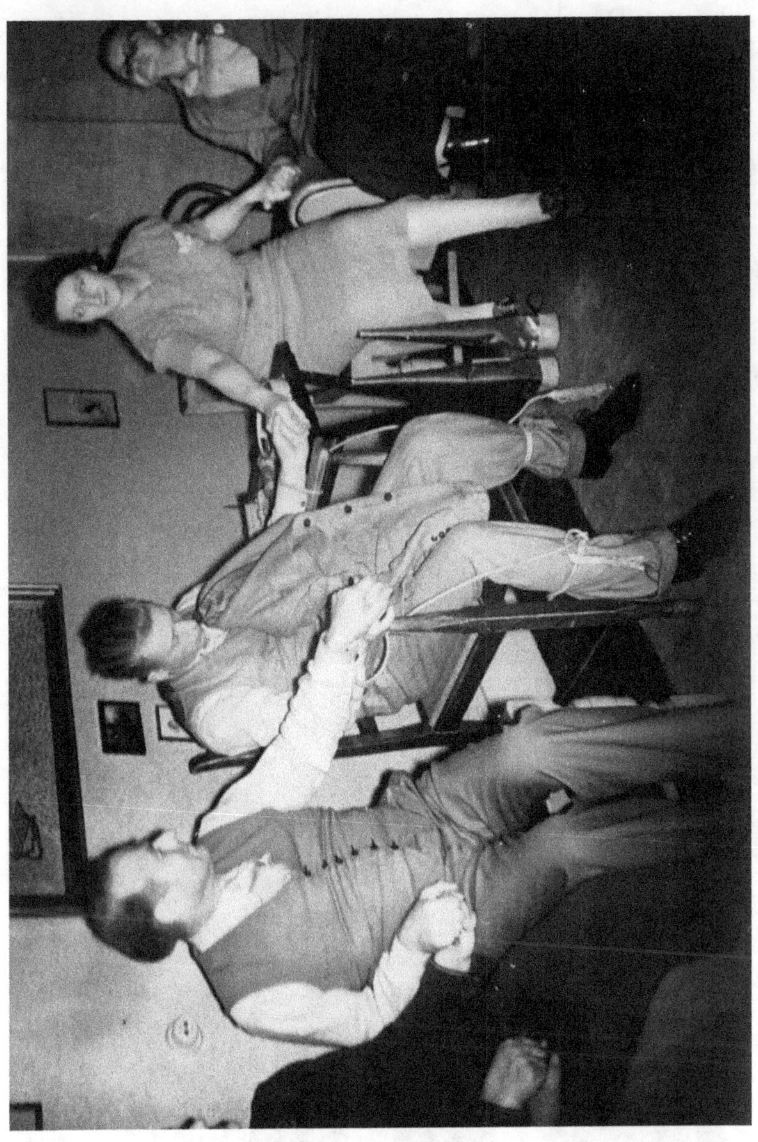

That same evening this was taken, showing a rare occasion when the sitters next to the medium were asked to hold his hands as the jacket was dematerialised, demonstrating that it had not passed over his hands as it did so. (A close-up was used as Plate 6 in Edwards' book.)

In December of that year Mr Stanley Croft, a member of the new Development Circle, took these of the ectoplasmic formations:

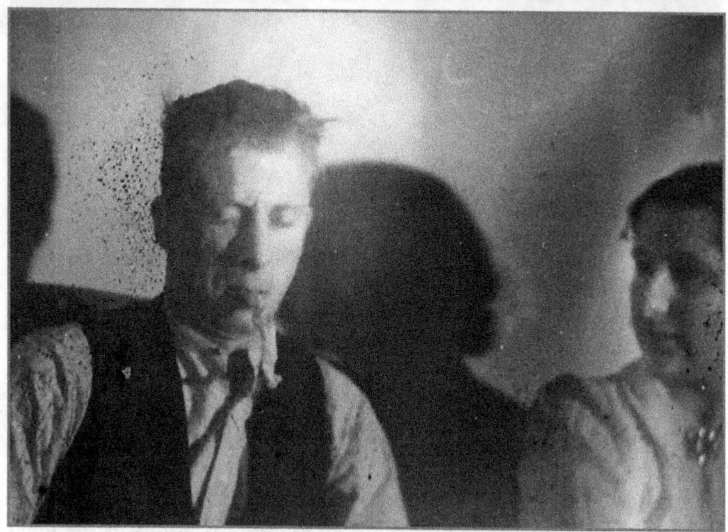

The black markings on the photograph above are probably due to poor washing in the development/ printing process.

Great care was taken in using light of any kind in the séances and the following statement was published by Harry Edwards in *The Two Worlds* in November 1938.

Under the heading of "Lights and Séances" in response to a previous letter from 'Investigator' who raised the point as to whether it is really wrong to expose a light in a physical circle or touch the manifestations or objects during or after levitation.

> "In sittings with Jack Webber, I have witnessed on two occasions incidents of this nature…on both occasions the offences were unintentional and committed without thought or design by the sitters who were both experienced Spiritualists. On the first occasion it was caused by the placing of a tambourine, that had been levitated to the knee of a sitter (Harry Boddington), back on to the floor causing a partial collapse of the medium and a haemorrhage. On this occasion the disturbance was relatively slight as even though blood was streaming from the medium's nose, he was still entranced and was able to proceed with the sitting although certain phenomena were no longer forthcoming.
>
> The second incident was more serious. By accident a flash from a torch pointed upwards into the room caused severe bleeding from the mouth and nose of the medium and the sitting had to be abandoned. Furthermore, the medium did not fully recover for several days. It is also noteworthy that every sitter I spoke to the following day was feeling, to some degree, the effects of the incident by tiredness and sickness. It should be obvious to the 'Investigator' that the return of the ectoplasmic rods that are in being during the séance to the medium immediately must have a detrimental effect.
>
> Another incident occurred during an event organized by 'The Link Association of Home Circles' (founded by Mr Noah Zerdin in the early 1930s). The séance was held

at the Rochester Square Temple where at least 300 people had gathered for this séance. Mrs Noah Zerdin laced the medium's coat securely through the buttonholes and another member of 'The Link' used his knowledge of knots and fastenings acquired in the Navy to rope Webber securely into his armchair. Yet at one point during the séance the medium's jacket was removed and hurled across the circle twelve feet away from where he was seated and later the lacings and knots were seen to be perfectly intact.

Mrs Street, president of the church located off Camden Road, London NW1, where the séance was held, was addressed through the trumpet by a Mrs Quiney, a former president of the church and "several other members of the audience received personal messages through the trumpet" writes Mr R. R. Yates, "but these conversations for the most part were carried on quietly by the spirit and its loved one in the audience so we could not always hear what was being said. This is the first time I have ever seen three trumpets simultaneously whirling around high in the air. The heights of the trumpets, on many occasions, was not less than ten feet from the floor and all three were operating independently of each other." Praise was given to the medium by Mr Yates who continued—saying "Before this critical audience, most of them Spiritualists and many experienced observers of psychic phenomena, Mr Webber gave abundant evidence of supernormal power."

However, this was not said before a member of the audience grabbed a trumpet from mid-air thus bringing to a sudden close an outstanding demonstration of physical mediumship. For when the light was switched on Jack Webber was found to be bleeding copiously from the nose and was too ill to resume."

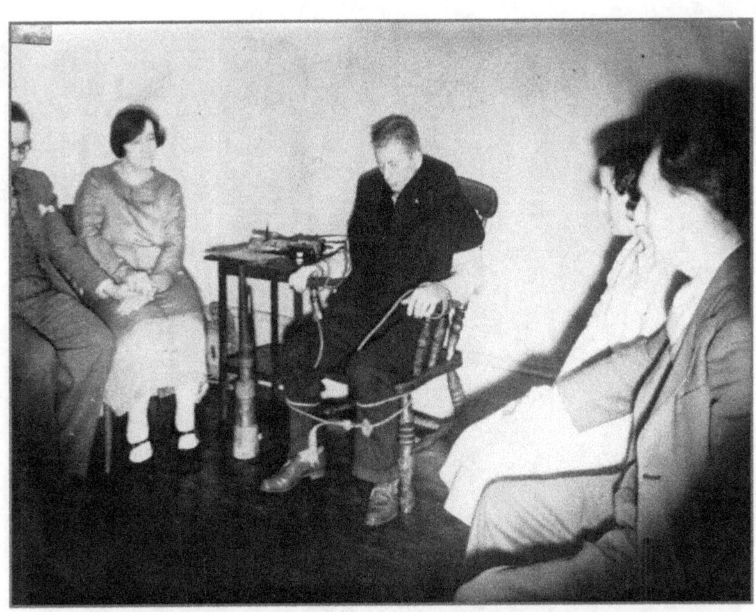

Note that these photographs were taken at different séances as the sitters are in different positions, but they show the progressive removal of the medium's jacket. Close-ups of these two photographs were used as Plates 3 & 4 in the original book. (Photographer Leon Isaacs)

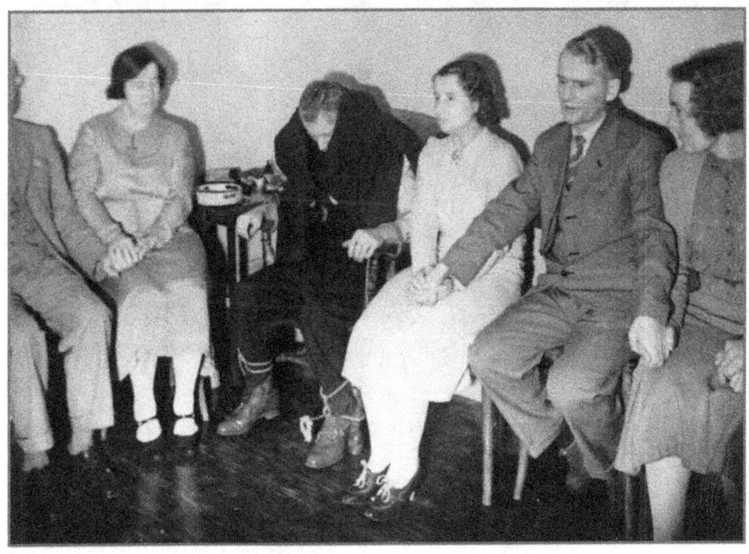

PSYCHIC NEWS

THE SPIRITUALIST NEWSPAPER WITH THE WORLD'S LARGEST CIRCULATION
(ON SALE EVERY THURSDAY)

LIFE AFTER DEATH PROVED

No. 339 LONDON: NOVEMBER 19, 1938 Price TWOPENCE
(Registered at the G.P.O. as a Newspaper)

SEANCE PICTURES THAT ARE A CHALLENGE TO SCIENCE

ALL THIS HAPPENED IN 14 SECONDS!

THESE photographs are a challenge to materialistic science, for they demonstrate what is regarded as the "impossible."

While the removal of a coat through ropes—this means that either the coat or the ropes dematerialised to allow matter to pass through matter—does not prove Survival, it proves the existence of a psychic law which materialists refuse to accept.

There is nothing religious about this demonstration, just as there is nothing religious about many of the "miracles" of the Bible.

For nearly a hundred years similar happenings have occurred at seances. When Spiritualists reported them they were usually met with incredulity.

Now, with the assistance of one of the latest discoveries of science, the infra-red ray, we can present these permanent records.

Jack Webber, a "physical medium," was securely roped to his chair, the knots being threaded with black cotton which normally should snap if interfered with.

Black cotton was also tied around a button and knotted through a button hole of his jacket, so that the slightest movement on his part would have broken them. Yet all these knots and threads were intact at the end of the seance!

The removal of the coat and its reappearance in its original position could not have been done by the medium. None of the sitters was responsible, as they were all controlled, everybody linking hands with his neighbour.

The feat was accomplished by an invisible intelligence. Whose was it?

The guides who spoke through the entranced medium, and through the trumpet in the direct voice, declared that they were responsible. This explanation fits the facts.

Conjuring is out of the question. No magician could have emulated this happening under the same conditions, nor at the speed with which it was accomplished—8 seconds for the coat's removal and 6 seconds for its replacement.

Fraud is out of the question.

Here the medium, Jack Webber, is seen lashed to his chair. Black cotton has been threaded around a button on his coat and through a button-hole and then knotted. This cotton would snap, in the ordinary course of events, if the coat were removed.

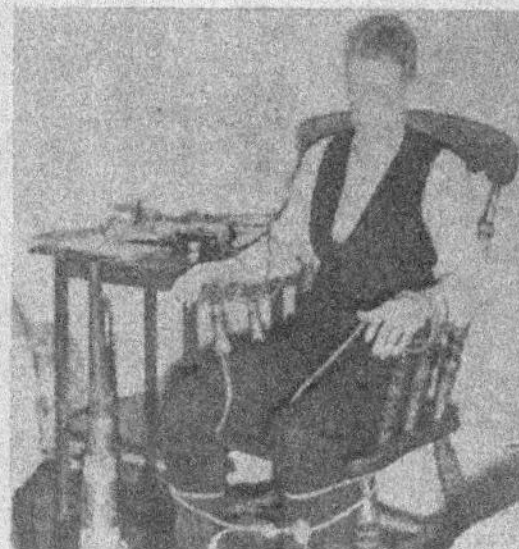

Eight seconds later. The medium's coat has been removed, but the knots and the ropes are left undisturbed. The sitters were allowed to examine the jacket, which still had the black cotton threaded around the button, through the button-hole and knotted as originally.

Six seconds later. You see the coat in the process of returning! It is half-way on the medium's body, the sleeves partially back in their original position. Part of the coat is semi-transparent, for waistcoat buttons can be seen through it.

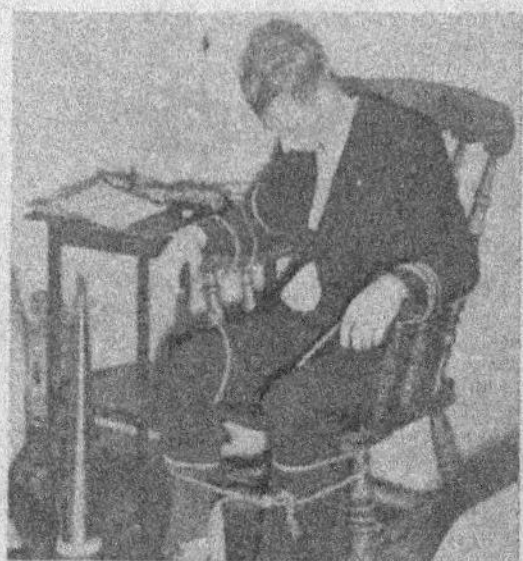

The jacket is now completely restored to its former position. All the lashings, knots and black cotton thread are intact—and in their original positions! Between the taking of these pictures the medium's guide asked for the white light to be put on!

These photographs were specially taken for "Psychic News" by Leon Isaacs. They are the copyright of the Fellowship of Spiritual Service, Balham, where the seance was held.

The photographs of the jacket removal were also used to promote the mediumship through 'Psychic News' as shown here on the Front page of November 19th 1938

(Printed with permission of Psychic News)

Chapter Five

1939 – Phenomena Challenged

In February/March 1939 Jack Webber's mediumship was brought into question with the accusation of fraud in connection with his physical mediumship being levelled at him during a séance organized through a Mr and Mrs Bell. The Bells, with a party from the Kent House Sanctuary in Beckenham, came in force with a preconceived plan to 'Frame up' and expose the medium. This was proved by the fact that Harry Edwards received a telephone warning from *Psychic News* of the group's intentions, on Tuesday, February 7th 1939, only a few hours before the sitting.

They came armed with torches to flash a beam of light on the medium, these were shown to Mr Edwards following the séance. To his knowledge only one of the group's members had previously sat with Jack Webber. The remainder including Mr and Mrs Bell came organized to condemn at all costs without any first-hand knowledge of the mediumship. Mr Edwards stressed in the invitation beforehand for any sitter to speak up if they had any doubts at any time during the séance. Not one word of doubt was uttered by any sitter throughout the séance. Mr Edwards pointed out several times during the séance, the human impossibility to accomplish that which everyone saw or experienced and there wasn't a murmur to the contrary. There were eighteen sitters on this occasion. Eleven of the Bells' party signed a prepared statement. They tried to get the independent sitters to also sign their document but none of them would.

What appeared to be their strategy took place during the roping of the medium. Two sitters were nominated to rope the medium. One person (un-associated with the party) tied the medium up tightly. The second person was one of the Bells' party, nominated by a Mrs Rolfe. As part of a pre-arranged plan, the ropes were deliberately left loose on one side, this in spite of the medium's request that the ropes around the arm be tied tighter, and that his upper arms be lashed to the back of the chair. At the end of the séance, Mrs Bell's first and immediate action was to go to the loose roping and point it out. She knew the arm that had been loosely roped, clearly proving the prearranged plan. Mrs Bell admitted the rapidity of the phenomena, white light being put on immediately after each experiment and before levitation of the trumpets. She said that this was not evidential.

The episode first came to the public domain when published in *The Two Worlds* on 17th February and carried on in *The Two Worlds* until 3rd March 1939. Much of the argument in favour of the medium was penned by Harry Edwards, however there were many letters printed from people who had had favourable sittings with Jack during and after that period. During the dispute Mr Edwards challenged Mrs Bell or her nominee to normally reproduce the same results. If she succeeded, he would pay £20.00 to the SNU Benevolent Fund: if she failed, she was to pay the same amount to the fund. (This offer was not taken up.)

Mrs Bell spoke of the un-evidential character of the direct voice. However, one person of her group openly confessed to wrongly accepting a name and purposely misleading the spirit voice with fictitious statements, but Mrs Bell still condemned the medium. She admitted the "features of the direct voice singing", but even in this she decried the medium.

Again, Mr Edwards challenged Mrs Bell or her nominee to reproduce similar singing through a trumpet with less than a half inch aperture in one end. "It is a physical impossibility," he stated. – Continuing that if it was indeed a fact that Mr Webber could produce normally, such a voice as produced in his séances, he would have no need to risk injury, for he could earn far more working in the safety of the concert halls.

Mr Edwards followed this with:

"In January and February of this year (1939) Mr Webber demonstrated before the London Spiritual Mission, London Spiritualist Brotherhood, Chelmsford Spiritualist Church, Great Metropolitan Spiritualist Association, London Spiritual Alliance Churches at Woodford, Harringay, Paddington, etc. At these gatherings many notable mediums and experienced Spiritualists were present. The editors of *Light, The Link* and sub-editor of *The Two Worlds* have also been present during these two months. Not one complaint had been received, all of these organisations have asked for more bookings.

On March 6th, Mr Webber is booked to demonstrate before members of the London District Council…in red light! Could he do this if not genuine? The following report and decision of the L.D.C. answers the underhand and malicious tactics of Mrs Bell's party. The infra-red photographs published in this and other countries of ectoplasmic formations etc., which are fraud-proof, should further reassure every reader. These photographs are evidence."

As part of his argument, Harry goes on to say,

"I am asking the editor to publish in this issue, a further report of this mediumship in red light. Here again, it shows fraud is an impossibility. I am also prepared, on behalf of Mr Webber, to accept any reasonable test sitting, judged by independent referees, that *Psychic News* or *The Two Worlds* cares to arrange. This, in itself, should be an answer to these irresponsible people."

This is that report:

"Séance in Red Light"

"In addition to the members of Mr Webber's home circle, the following were present at the séance reported below: Mr Leon Isaacs (*Psychic News* photographer), Mr Dedine along with two of his colleagues holding Government posts, all of whose integrity is beyond reproach.

The séance with Jack Webber reported below, was held prior to March 3rd, 1939 and red light was on for the whole of the séance, so that what happened was visible to the eyes of each sitter present; the following phenomena occurred:

Levitation of trumpet in slow and violent motion, levitation of the medium roped to his chair, full length materialized forms appeared.

The Guide said he would de-materialize the medium and in good red light, before everyone's eyes, we saw the head, hands and wrists vanish, leaving just the medium's clothes sitting in the chair. It remained so for approximately one minute. They all then saw the rapid re-emergence of the medium back into his suit once more.

Mr Edward's hand was taken hold of by a hand and placed on the medium's hand. A similar action was taken with the sitter on the other side of the medium. Where did these hands come from? Even though red light was on for the duration of the séance at times white light was also put on to show more clearly such things as the roping of the medium to the chair.

After the white light was switched off, with their hands on the medium's hands, the coat was taken clear off the body. The coat did not pass over the hands – an impossible human feat. The white light was put on immediately showing Mr Webber still roped in. Again, the white light was extinguished, with their hands still holding those of the medium he was taken out of the ropes and the chair and left standing in the middle of the circle. Within a few seconds he was back in the chair and in the ropes, as originally tied."

The Two Worlds published an Editorial providing complete vindication of Mr Webber's mediumship and is worthy of mention within these pages as testimony to the fairness in the examination of this case.

"The Webber Case"

"The question of fraud in connection with physical mediumship is a very serious one; but it is one which must be seen in its proper perspective. We have to recognize firstly that the phenomena which occur at such séances in many cases contradict the accepted scientific theories of the day. To a scientist it is impossible to suppose that a heavy object like a table can be raised a foot into the air without actual contact of some physical kind; yet it repeatedly happens in the séance room. The first thought of the scientist on observing it is that his senses might have deceived him; his second that some wilful act has been performed by someone present for the purpose of deceiving him. The last thing the scientific mind will admit, as a rule, is that it is the presence of an unknown law or a new form of energy. We had a call recently from a middle-aged man who has been engaged all his life in scientific work. He had attended a séance with Mrs Duncan, he had seen materialized forms in good light, and he said to me "As a scientist I know these things cannot occur; as a man I know they did occur. Where am I?"

That is the attitude of a scientific mind when phenomena occur in the light. When, however, they occur under the cover of darkness, where his sense of sight cannot operate, imagination tends to invent explanations. It cannot be denied that nine tenths of the accusations made during the history of this Movement have arisen from phenomena which occurred in the dark. With mediums such as D.D. Home, George Spriggs, Walter Jeune, John Taylor and a few others we could mention, no serious question was ever raised concerning their mediumship, at least not until after they had passed away. Then, people were content to criticize, not the phenomena but the records left by witnesses. It is not difficult to find flaws in such records, if only because some of the details were considered too unimportant for recording.

The Editor and Secretary of *The Two Worlds,* Mr Ernest Oaten, then goes on to say that the question of the dark séance has always been the bugbear of Spiritualism and will continue to be so. Investigators, finding that they cannot trust their own observations in the dark, think they are equally to distrust not only the medium but the sitters. To be perfectly candid, I have found more attempts to practice deception in the dark room by sitters than I have by mediums.

Now it cannot be denied that physical phenomena takes place more readily in the dark and in the home circle where all the sitters are known to one another, and have confidence in one another, there may be valid reasons for the dark séance but it is quite another question as to whether Spiritualism has benefitted or been hindered by professional mediumship exercised in the dark. Certainly, the scientific mind can evolve safeguards of various type which impose a check upon the phenomena which happens, but this implies rigid control by the experimenters.

Let us come, however, to the question at issue of Mr Webber. The first communication we received in this controversy was from Mr Edwards, which we published a fortnight ago. The policy of *The Two Worlds* has always been that it is wise to allow both parties to a dispute to express themselves; and I therefore wrote to Mrs Bell so that I could publish the two statements together. Since then, many letters have rolled into this office from people who have sat with Mr Webber. Outside the members of Mrs Bell's party, only one of them has questioned Mr Webber's mediumship. Many of them have had sittings with him in their own homes, where they have provided their own conditions. I have also interviewed several people who sat with him in the Provinces, many of them Spiritualists of wide experience. In each case they have been absolutely certain of the genuineness of Mr Webber's mediumship. My assistant, Mr Hicks, sat with him personally last month and after careful examination of the statements of Mrs Bell and Mrs Rolfe, stigmatizes them as being ridiculous, considering his own experiences with Webber. In fact, the overwhelming testimony of those who have sat with Jack Webber (many of them have sat many times) is that there is not a shred of foundation for the charge of fraud.

Let us look at the question from another angle. Mrs Bell and her party admittedly had made up their minds that Mr Webber was fraudulent before they attended the séance and the object of their sitting was to expose what they considered a form of fraud which was injuring the movement they were interested in. Now, a mind made up is not the right attitude in which to go to a séance. I assert, from a long experience, that it is not difficult to compel a medium who is in a sensitive state or trance state to do things which he would never dream of doing except under the pressure of suggestion. There is no place on earth where the actions of the mind have greater potency than in a physical séance! Sitting some time ago with Mrs Duncan, her guide "Albert" warned us "I want you to remember that my medium is in a sensitive, hypnotic state, and if any of you sitters give orders, don't be surprised if she obeys them. Please, therefore, refrain from direct instructions and leave that to me. Ask questions if you will, but don't give orders." That was very wise advice.

The fact that a séance is held in the dark often gives rein to the imagination of the sitters. Quite a lot of credulous people see wonderful phenomena which does not occur, while others see fraud which is not there. It is a case of the mind attempting to put an interpretation on certain happenings when there is not enough scope for the observation to determine what actually occurs. This, it seems to me, is the position of Mrs Bell. In a condition of uncertainty, she has interpreted certain happenings in the terms of her own preconceptions. In analysing her report and that of Mrs Rolfe, I can find nothing but opinions, based upon their interpretation of certain happenings. In a word, it seems to me that suspicion, rather than fact, has been the ground for accusation. The photographs which *The Two Worlds* has published from time to time concerning Mr Webber's mediumship, allied with the corroborative reports of scores of people who have sat with him at different times and under different conditions, leaves no shred of doubt in my mind that supernormal phenomena do occur in Mr Webber's presence.

One great good, however, has emerged from the controversy: Mr Webber is now sitting in red light, where his own actions and those of the sitters can be observed. That is a tremendous benefit. Every effort should be made by professional mediums to dispense with darkness as the phenomena have and can be obtained in the red light; it only needs further development. Why a red light? I suppose the idea of a red light is based upon the fact that photographic plates are less sensitive to red light than to daylight, but it does not all follow that because silver salts are less liable to be influenced by red than white light, that this applies to psychic force."

Letters in support of Jack Webber's mediumship continued to arrive at the offices of, and be published by *The Two Worlds* for several weeks following this controversy. His work now went from strength to strength through continuing to hold his séances in lighted conditions. The following is a report published in *Psychic News* during June 1939, entitled "Materialised Form Seen in Red Light", which shows the rapid improvements being brought about in Jack's development:

> "In red light, a full form materialised at Jack Webber's developing circle last week and held his arms and hands to the light for all to see. The Guide asked for the red light, which is rheostat controlled, to be lowered. This was done, but it was not dim enough for the Guide's purpose. A pair of hands or grippers, covered with ectoplasm, took hold of the light fitting and pulled it down. The red light was then turned on and off by Spirit power, a switch in the fitting being used. Soon the light was shown with ectoplasm around it, dimming the radiance of the light. A second form materialised, and the red lamp was lifted, switched on, and the light taken to the face of the materialised form, showing it clearly from various positions. Later, ectoplasmic material was shown stretching from the medium's mouth to the floor, where it spread out for several feet. The two sitters on each side of the medium were asked to hold the ectoplasm, to unfold it and stretch it out. It took the two people with the full extent of their arms to unfold it. The rapidity with which this considerable area of ectoplasmic substance was withdrawn back into the medium was remarkable. The gulping sound from the medium indicated throat

> action, but the amazing speed with which the ectoplasm was reabsorbed makes the theory of regurgitation absurd. To the touch, this ectoplasmic material felt like a very close and finely woven silk. It was damp and possessed a peculiar odour. While Mr Webber's further development is being conducted in red light, he is not yet able to work in red light in the séances undertaken elsewhere."

In April 1939 the renamed Balham Psychical Research Society, headed by Harry Edwards, arranged for a Jack Webber séance to be held at the London studios of the Decca Record company to record Jack's Guide, *Reuben*, singing. Several attempts to record *Reuben's* powerful voice were carried out and eventually the trumpet, used to project the voice, had to be moved away from the microphone by some ten feet to avoid distortion of the recording. In those days, of course, it was 78 rpm brittle Shellac records that were the method used for recording music which is probably the reason for the rarity of this important record today. The home circle members were all present for this momentous occasion and my Grandparents' (Jim and Nellie Evans) voices can be heard clearly in the background of each song, singing descant to *Reuben*. Two songs were recorded, one to each side of the record; *Lead Kindly Light* and *There's A Land*, both songs were regularly sung at church services. *Reuben*, however, had a favourite song that he would have liked to have recorded, this was Danny Boy but after several failed attempts at the studios that tune had to be abandoned. Thankfully the recording of *Lead Kindly Light* and *There's A Land* is now available on Youtube at: Youtube.com/watch?v=ppEyMjXrUlg [1]

At the end of the first song you can hear a closing prayer and thanks from *Black Cloud* (Jack's doorkeeper) and at the end of each recording you will distinctly hear the aluminium séance trumpet, through which he was singing, fall to the floor.

---

1. NB. Please note the case of each letter if you wish to listen to it.

The record was available to buy at the time, through Balham Psychical Research Society, for the princely sum of six shillings and sixpence. Harry Edwards stated in his book about Jack's Mediumship:

> "A feature of Mr Webber's Mediumship is the singing of hymns and ballads through the trumpet or in the independent voice. One control, *Reuben*, possesses an extremely powerful voice, so strong that at times the trumpet is in a condition of tension, setting up such a high vibration that it takes on a ringing tone. At all times the direct voice is of full loud-speaker strength, possessing a quality of tone that is distinctive, and which the medium is incapable of reproducing. Each syllable is clearly articulated. If the medium could produce this singing voice normally, he could obtain a good living on the concert platform without endangering his life and health at public séances."

The original label was bright yellow

“In the Sweet by and by” (or “There's a land”)

There's a land that is fairer than day,
And by faith we can see it afar,
For the Loved Ones wait over the way,
To prepare us a dwelling place there.

Chorus:
In the sweet by and by,
We shall meet on the beautiful shore,
In the sweet by and by
We shall meet on the beautiful shore.

Next verse:
To our bountiful Father above,
We will offer our tribute of praise,
For the glorious gift of His love,
And the blessings that hallow our days
Chorus:

“Lead Kindly Light”

Lead, kindly light, amidst th’ encircling gloom
Lead Thou me on!
The night is dark, and I am far from home—
Lead Thou me on!
Keep Thou my feet; I do not ask to see
The distant scene—one step, enough for me

I was not ever thus, nor prayed that Thou
Shouldst lead me on:
I loved to choose and see my path, but now
Lead Thou me on!
I loved the garish day, and, spite of fears
Pride ruled my will; Remember not past years.

Within a few days of the sitting on February 7th and the ensuing drama, Leon Isaacs was due to take more photos and asked Sir William Neil Connor, better known as the *Daily Mirror* reporter 'Cassandra', to transport him and the equipment to Childebert Road for the sitting.

This resulted in a 2-page report in the *Daily Mirror* on February 28th 1939, well reported in the original book, but what was not shown in that report was the complete photograph, where we see the table, weighing 45lbs, suspended in mid-air with books levitating off the table and landing on the sitters' laps. Two other photographs were taken that evening, the first one taken is shown below.

Here the trumpet is seen balanced by the covered window on its narrow end (taken by Daily Mirror Photographer)

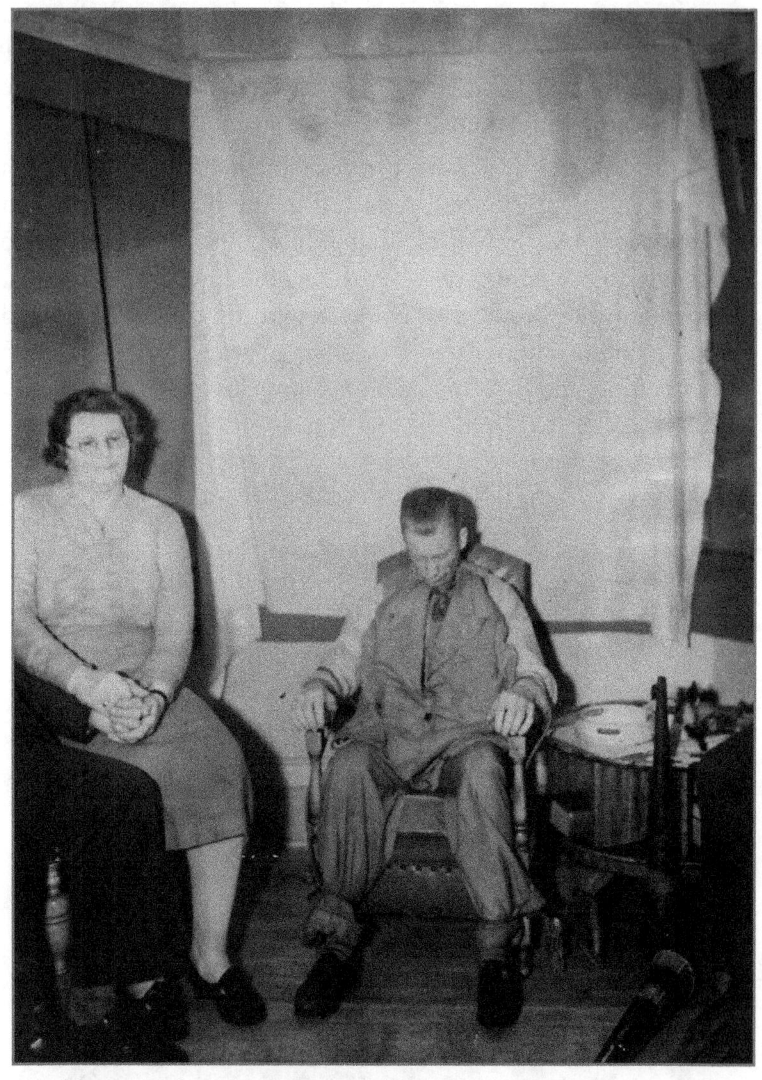

In this second photograph of the evening. The medium's jacket has been removed from his body without his bindings being released.
Note the position of the table before the following photograph was taken.

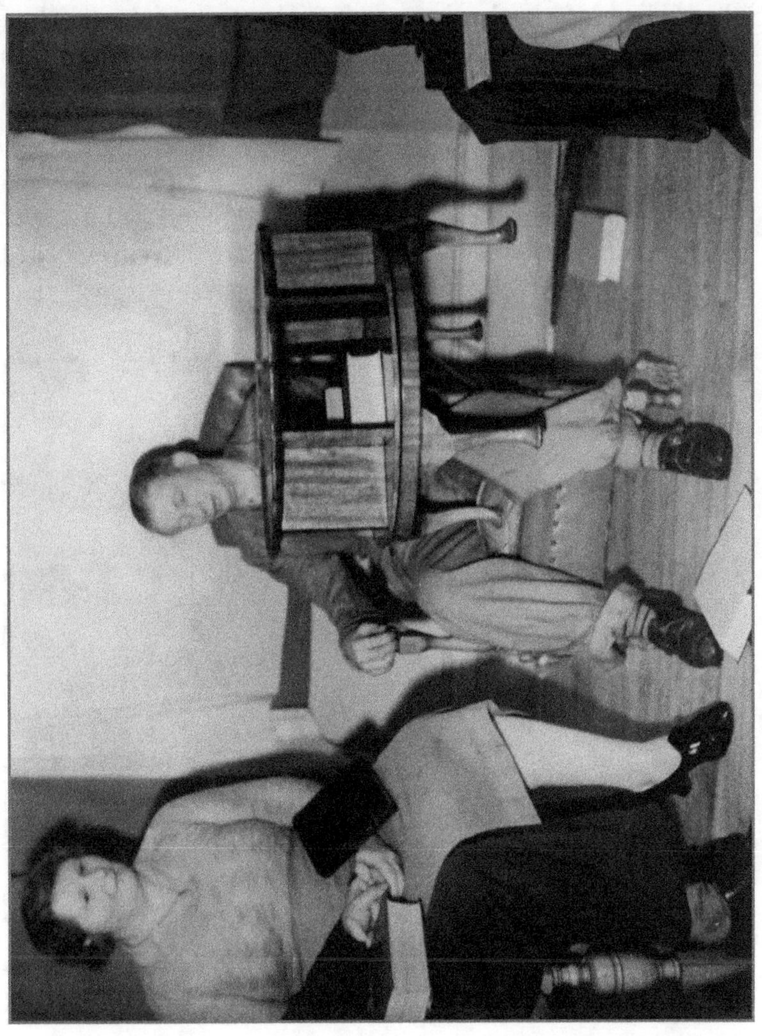

This third photograph of the evening has been rotated to give maximum enlargement so that you might appreciate the position of the sitters, the table and the three books levitating towards the sitters. One to the right and two to the left. A further book is landing on the floor at the medium's feet. The levitated table weighed 45lbs - 20kgs (photo taken by Daily Mirror Photographer, Leon Isaacs)

It may be noticed in the photograph on the previous page that the medium's jacket has been replaced by the spirit team before this was taken. This did not always occur and the jacket was frequently found elsewhere in the room.

In December 1939 Leon Isaacs took the following two photographs of the fine ectoplasmic 'gauze' stretched out over the medium's head to the wall. These have been published before but not in their largely uncropped state.

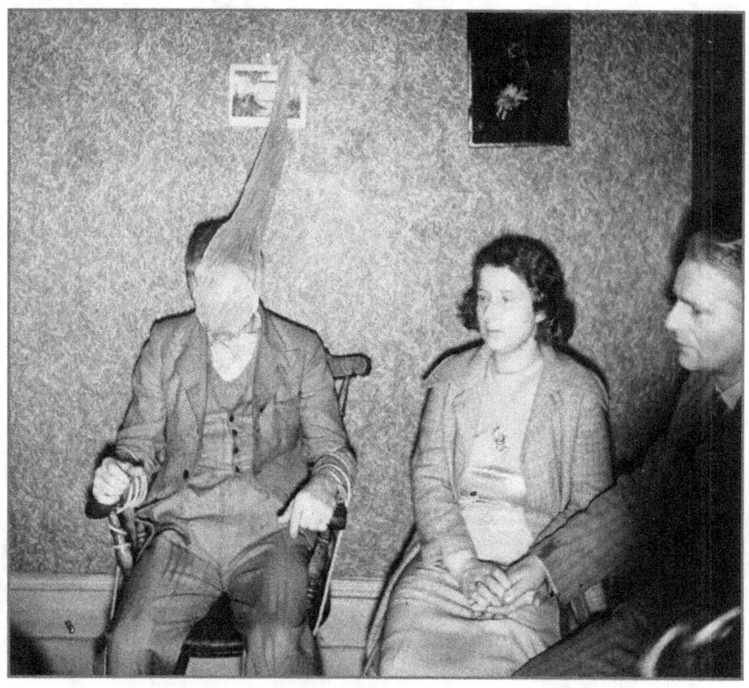

First of the exposures showing ectoplasm flowing from the mouth to be suspended from the edge of a picture on the wall above his head.
This also shows a good photo of Rhoda, Jack's wife who usually sat beside him in the circle. Harry Edwards is to the left of Rhoda. (To allow greater magnification, the left edge of the original has been cropped as it contained only dark walls.)

Ectoplasm stretched up to the wall behind the medium, taken from a different angle.

In the previous illustration the two people to the extreme left are my Nan and Grampa, Nellie and Jim Evans. Jim had been Jack's circle leader from the early days and continued to be so throughout the time in London. Below is an enlargement from the previous photograph.

Nellie and Jim Evans 1939

Chapter Six

The Apported Egyptian Amulet

The production of apports had occured throughout Jack Webber's mediumship. Their method of arrival demonstrated that apported objects may come via the medium's body. This is consistent with those apport mediums who produce apports using a trumpet for their delivery.

Harry Edwards explains in his book *The Mediumship of Jack Webber* that the trumpet is connected to the medium by an ectoplasmic arm/rod. The apport in its dematerialized condition travels via the medium's body, along the ectoplasmic appendage into the mouth of the trumpet where it is materialized; the trumpet acting as a conserver or retainer for the ectoplasmic force and the act of materialisation.

On one occasion in 1939 the apporting of two objects was witnessed in red light. For some hours before a séance when apports may occur, Jack would feel a tightness of the abdomen and was therefore able, at times, to know what was intended. On the occasion referred to, he had this sensation and therefore he invited a search to be made of his person in the séance room before the start of procedures.

This was carried out by Mr Stanley Croft, a member of the Metropolitan Police Force and a member of the new circle, in view of all the sitters and prior to Jack being roped to his chair.

The red light was on, it was sufficiently bright enough for all to see the medium bound to the chair. Trumpets were in levitation, also clearly discernible in the red light. One of these turned around, presenting its large end to Jack's solar plexus (mid-torso) area and an object was heard to fall into it. It then came across to Harry Edwards who was instructed to take the article from inside the trumpet—an Egyptian Amulet. After a minute or two the trumpet again travelled to Jack's solar plexus area and another object was heard to fall into it.

This time the trumpet went across to Stanley Croft who removed a small stone carving of a Buddha. Both items were photographed and are presented in Plate 12 of *The Mediumship of Jack Webber.*

Neither of these objects were found during the very thorough search of Jack carried out by Mr Croft earlier. Furthermore, all eleven persons present in the séance saw the medium tied to the chair and the trumpet, which seconds before had been in very forceful and intense levitation, move to the medium's body. At this point the article was heard to fall into the trumpet. Ectoplasm was not seen at the time of the séance since the process was being executed in red light and it apparently tends to be at its strongest form or highest vibration when invisible. Ray Branch, in his book on the life story of Harry Edwards, stresses that of all the accolades and personal gifts received from patients and admirers throughout his years as a healer, there was one small object which Harry came to treasure more than any of his earthly possessions, and that was an apport received through Jack Webber – the Egyptian Amulet.

Soon after the object was received, Harry took it to the British Museum for examination. He was told that it was made from Theban glass, that it was 3500 years old and that the hieroglyphic message showed that it was made for the "Custodian of the Gate of the Southern Countries" who may have, in all probability, been one of the Pharaohs.

Upon his passing, Harry's sister, Ivy, gave the amulet to Ray Branch who had taken on the mantle of running 'The

Healing Sanctuary' at Burrows Lea, in Harry's stead. Subsequently upon Ray's passing it became part of his estate and was bequeathed to his son Clive for future safe keeping. Fortunately, Clive is still in close contact with the Healing Sanctuary and it was through their records and personnel that I was able to trace and contact him for the purpose of viewing this little gem once again and for being able to photograph it for inclusion in this book.

The Egyptian Amulet with £1 coin for size comparison.
(see back cover for first ever full colour representation of this object)

The excitement of seeing the amulet once again got my juices flowing and created within me the desire to research its authenticity and to have it confirmed once more by various authoritative and learned experts in our country's museums. Photos and particulars relating to the amulet were sent to Liverpool's World Museum which has world class knowledge of Ancient Egyptian artefacts. It was also sent once again to the British Museum's Department of Egyptology in London.

Both of these fine establishments came back with their findings which were that it is not 3500 years old. It transpires therefore that when it was apported into the séance room it was relatively new. It is likely that more years have passed since it was apported in 1939 than its age at the moment it was brought through Jack Webber's trumpet and presented to Harry Edwards. Although its veracity as an ancient Egyptian Amulet leaves us somewhat bemused, it is still a fact – and probably the most important fact – that it is a genuine apport, and is well documented. That to my mind is far more important than its age or authenticity as an antiquity.

However, the design and the artistry of this, in no doubt beautiful creation, even though it may have been mass produced for the Grand Tour market, does have its own merits. And I believe it is worth describing and imparting the details of some of these little-known elements to the reader!

Imprinted around the edge of the amulet are various hieroglyphs which both Liverpool and London museums said didn't make sense. However, after a lot of investigation on-line I eventually came across a reproduction of a wall painting from a tomb discovered before 1828. Obviously, had the tomb been discovered after 1939, the time when the amulet was apported, then the question of its authenticity may have been ponderable. However, the artwork likely to have been used to help create the amulet was in existence, and in the public domain, at that time.

In 1926, Nina de Garis Davies and Alan Gardiner published the complete description of the tomb under the auspices of the Egypt Exploration Society: *The tomb of Huy, Viceroy of Nubia in the reign of Tutankhamun* and within it they reproduced some of the artwork provided by Nestor l'Hôte, the French Egyptologist, painter and graphic artist, who had previously visited the tomb and reproduced the wall paintings that are almost gone today (*see opposite*).

The wall-painting scene depicted on the Amulet.
(the colour view of wall painting is reproduced on the back cover).

This enlargement of the amulet shows the hieroglyphs quite clearly. The dimensions and weight of the original are 45mm high x 35mm wide at the base x 5mm thick x 60 grams

One of the more interesting discoveries I made was that only one Pharaoh has ever been depicted holding the Flail and Crook in the left hand and the Ankh in the right – as indicated on the amulet and in the painting. These are royal insignia. The Crook denotes Kingship, while the Flail stands for fertility of the land, and the Ankh is the symbol of Life. The Pharaoh sitting on the throne wearing a Khepresh (head-dress) which is a blue war crown, depicts the image of Tutankhamun. His tomb was discovered in 1922 and his considerable popularity may also have contributed to the creation of this souvenir piece.

Interpretation of the hieroglyphs is another matter but there is a solid link between Tutankhamun and Amenhotep (also called Huy). Huy was Viceroy of Nubia (at the time of Tutankhamun) and this relates to the description allotted to the amulet back in 1939 by the British Museum when they suggested it was made for the "Custodian of the Gate of the Southern Countries". That is exactly what Huy's title and relationship to Tutankhamun commanded and the hieroglyphs on the amulet appear to depict this (in part). The glyphs down the left edge, from the top, individually translate as:

1. Fettered or tied to. 2.Vizier in the South. 3. Water (of/by). 4. All/Every. 5. Desert/Foreign Country. 6. Forever. 7. No.11. The glyphs down the right individually translate as: L. Border of Land. 2. Together with. 3.Great Holy. 4.Attained/Appointed. 5. F or V 6. W/U. 7. Offering. 8. In the name of God. 9. Take possession.

Needless to say, it would take an expert in the study of hieroglyphic text to be able to correctly interpret the meanings in the way they are intended to be read. Especially as they are from a language written around 1800 years before the birth of Jesus.

The story does not finish there. With my curiosity piqued I wasn't wholly satisfied that such a beautiful little masterpiece could potentially be the work of a back-street-glass maker in an Egyptian bazaar during the early 1900s. So, I took it upon myself to ask the question of one of those who was present at the time the amulet was materialised into existence during a Jack Webber séance.

On Sunday December 8th, 2019, I attended, along with other family members and friends, our Christmas Home Circle during which family and friends from the Spirit World join with us through the deep trance mediumship of my younger sister, to share Christmas greetings and salutations. I had the opportunity to speak on this occasion with my Grampa, Jim Evans, Jack's circle leader throughout his development and time in London. Amongst other things I asked him whether the amulet was indeed an authentic piece from the time of Tutankhamun or whether it had been a tourist piece from the bazaars of Egypt. He confirmed it was a tourist piece and was not from a tomb of one of the pharaohs. He said they (spirit) would not be allowed, or even wish, to remove and keep grave goods. Only lost and unwanted items are removed, apported, and left with us.

As an example, he likened it to a time when Jack's Guide, *Black Cloud* apported his Tomahawk into the home development circle with damp earth still clinging to it. This precious object was taken away again shortly afterwards and asported back to the place from where it had come.

The Amulet is made from glass which can clearly be seen on the obverse side where there is a small bit of damage in the bottom right hand corner. Both sides of the amulet have the same design with both images facing in the same direction. They are, however, not identical which indicates the method of manufacture was probably via a mould rather than a stamped impression.

Chapter Seven

Jack Webber Mediumship Investigated

The following detail is taken from the Quarterly Journal of the I.I.P.I. (International Institute of Psychic Investigation) and relates to work carried out by well-known Psychic Investigator Mr B. Abdy Collins C.I.E. in early 1940.

The main thrust of his work refers to Harry Edwards and his book entitled *The Mediumship of Jack Webber*. Collins goes on to comment that one has to remember that the manuscript was in the hands of Edwards' printers in January 1940, just two months before the medium's sudden passing. The book, he felt, was intended as a challenge to those who could not accept the facts described within and for the sceptics to come and test the mediumship for themselves. He considered that neither was it supposed to be a final summing up of all that could ever be accomplished through Jack Webber and as things turned out it would be unfair of anyone to blame Mr Edwards on this score. Most of the phenomena produced by the famous physical mediums of the past was claimed, by Edwards, for Jack Webber and possibly even some hitherto unknown. He backs up his descriptions by a series of photographs taken partly by himself and other members of the Balham Psychic Research Society and partly by Leon Isaacs, well-known photographer employed by the *Daily Mirror*...some of which are laid out within this chapter.

This was the era of an invention called Infra-Red Photography which allowed that which was being produced in the dark of the séance room to be witnessed, as though being photographed in daylight.

The series of photographic plates included in Harry Edwards' book were quite unique of their time and remain some of the best attested to records of physical phenomena ever produced. These were selected as being the best examples of the different types of phenomena through Jack's mediumship. However, other photographs do exist, but they weren't considered necessarily good enough for inclusion in the final publication of Harry's book. As in previous chapters, the following pages contain more of those photographs of Jack Webber's mediumship and phenomena not previously used for publication. Some due to the poor quality of the photograph,[1] but I believe these "also rans" are still extremely interesting to study and I believe form a more complete record of that short period in Jack's mediumship in London, so I include them within this publication as they are worthy of viewing by those interested in this subject.

If the phenomena were not genuine then either Mr Edwards invented or greatly exaggerated them or else Mr Webber effected them by trickery or the aid of accomplices. Accomplices can be ruled out as in a large percentage of the sittings which the mediums gave all over the country, he is said to have travelled alone and often arrived only just before the séance. This is a matter to which Collins can bear testimony in one instance and the evidence of Mr Case, President of the Cambridge Psychical Research Society is cited as confirmation in another case. In many of the lone sittings some of the most striking phenomena occurred yet some people will see "accomplices" everywhere if there is anything for which they cannot account. At a sitting at Walton House, Walton Street,

1. With today's Photoshop technology some of the original 80-year-old photographs have been given a little more brightness or contrast for this publication but absolutely NO other changes have been made to them. (AH Publisher)

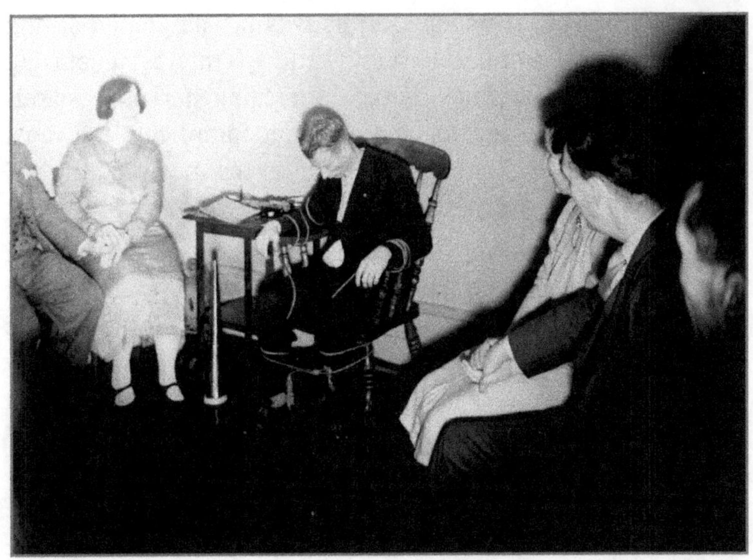

The Infra-red exposure above shows the medium roped to his chair. According to the original records, just <u>five seconds</u> later the photo below was taken, showing the medium and his chair being levitated. The rapid movement is shown by the blurring. (Photos by Leon Isaacs)

in London SW3, at which Collins was in charge and sitting next to the medium, relatively little of interest occurred. Yet a sitter sending in a letter expressing her impressions wrote "There seemed to be several accomplices, the most obvious being the stouter gentleman on the medium's right." That person was Abdy Collins!

That Mr Edwards is not inventing or exaggerating everything is proved by the testimony of independent witnesses quoted in his book, but the greater part of it consists of statements made by the author himself, unsupported by evidence other than the photographs, of which nine were taken by himself and others by his associates. Due to Mr Edwards' personal investment in the sponsorship of the medium, Collins, not unnaturally, concluded that Edwards must have had a financial interest in the mediumship or received some *quid pro quo* for his services to the medium. It was stated by Harry Edwards that he received no financial support from this venture, and this was very recently[2] corroborated by his daughter, in a letter to me, suggesting that no money had changed hands as a result of Jack's seances. If we accept these statements it adds very materially to the value of the book. Mr McCulloch one of the amateur photographers, also assured Collins that his photographs represent a substantial outlay of his time and money. As it is inconceivable that the members of the Balham Society have sat so many times with Webber under their own conditions and been deceived by him, it is obvious that this book deserves serious attention of all those interested in psychical research.

Let us now turn to some of the more important phenomena and the evidence for them. Abdy Collins advises that he sat with Webber on four occasions. At these sittings and apparently at many others a circle of fifteen to twenty people

---

2. Letter received in January 2019

would sit around the room. Webber was roped securely in his chair by one or two of the sitters. His arms were tied with varying degrees of 'tightness' to the arms of the chair and his legs to the chair legs, but his hands themselves were left free from below the wrists and were not held except on particular events. The other sitters joined hands with each other, except those next to the medium who clasped the hand of the person next to them with both hands.

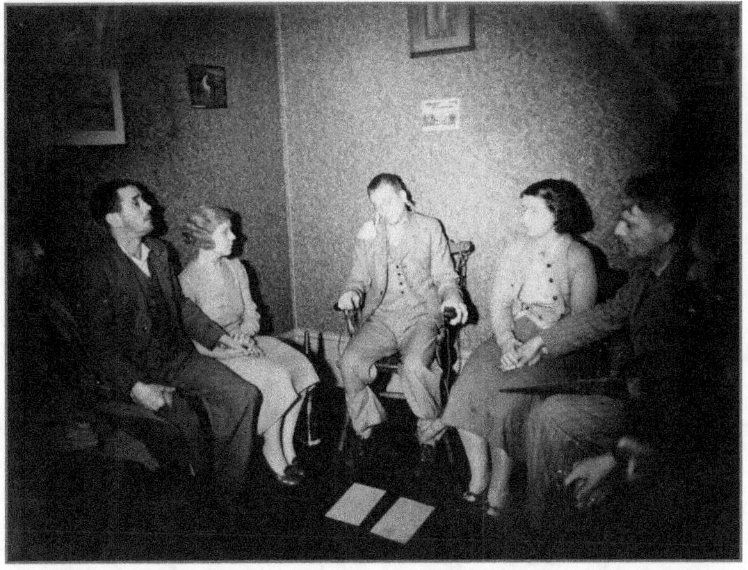

This infrared photograph shows the sitters next to the medium with both of their hands in the hand of the next sitter. This is commonly used as a precaution for protection of the medium and to rule out any complicity in the phenomena.
An enlargement of the medium showing the flow of ectoplasm from his ears was used as Plate 24 in 'The Mediumship of Jack Webber'

If it were possible for the medium to free himself after the light was turned out (sittings were usually in the dark) and get back again before it was turned on, then he may have been able to cause many but I think not all of the phenomena by normal means. The sceptic will say that any clever conjurer can manage this under these conditions. It will be seen, however, that some of those who tied him up claim special knowledge of knot tying and deny that the medium could have escaped from their special knots.

Collins sat next to, or next but one to, the medium three times and observed the ropes and knots very closely. On one occasion at Walton House the light was turned off and on seven times during the seventy-five minutes in the séance room and every time the medium was found tightly bound to the chair and the original knots where undisturbed. Phenomena started just after the light was turned off and ceased just before it was turned on. He claims to have also seen the medium, by the light of a phosphorescent article, sitting bound to his chair while another article was floating in the air. Many others have born witness to the same experience. It is further known that the medium sat in good red light so all could witness his position in the chair and while infra-red photographs were taken[3], they would show the medium always bound in his chair while the various phenomena are occurring.

Certainly, to the sceptics many of the photographs may look suspicious or faked, if only because they will probably be contrary to their preconceived notions of what they ought to be. Moreover, the trumpets in some cases appear to be supported by the sitters, what might appear to be intended for ectoplasmic rods supporting them may look like cotton-wool etc. The *bone fides* of the photographers are therefore of great importance. On this count, Collins wrote to Mr Leon Isaacs who took sixteen out of the thirty-five photographs in the book and asked him whether he was satisfied with the conditions under which his photographs were taken. He kindly replied at some length. While he cannot guarantee that some of the effects might not have been obtained normally by Webber

3. In his book, Edwards writes of this in particular regard to the photos of the ectoplasm over the medium's head shown at the end of the previous chapter.

himself or some of the sitters who were uncontrolled, he has no reason to suspect it and feels quite sure that a large amount, if not all, of the phenomena are genuine.

The evidence for ectoplasm, which is copiously illustrated, also seems strong. Mr McCullough told Collins that some of the plates have been enlarged several times for the book and as a result show no signs of textile/fabric. Various sitters have described it as "closely woven silk of a rich quality" and on other occasions "like wet toy balloon rubber" etc. Mr Isaacs did not handle it himself, though as will be seen he took several pictures of it, but he was told by various sitters that they handled it and watched in good red light as it disappeared into the medium.

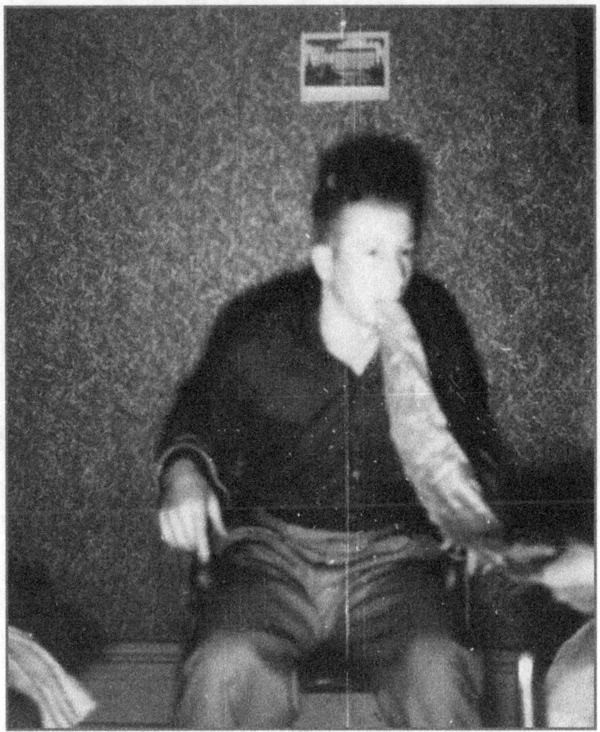

Here in a previously unpublished photo a sitter handles the ectoplasm flowing from Jack's mouth.

Left:* *Taken shortly before the previous photo, fine shiny silk-like ectoplasm flows from Jack's mouth.

Gossamer fine ectoplasmic 'cloth' flows from Jack's mouth. Note the proximity of the sitters.

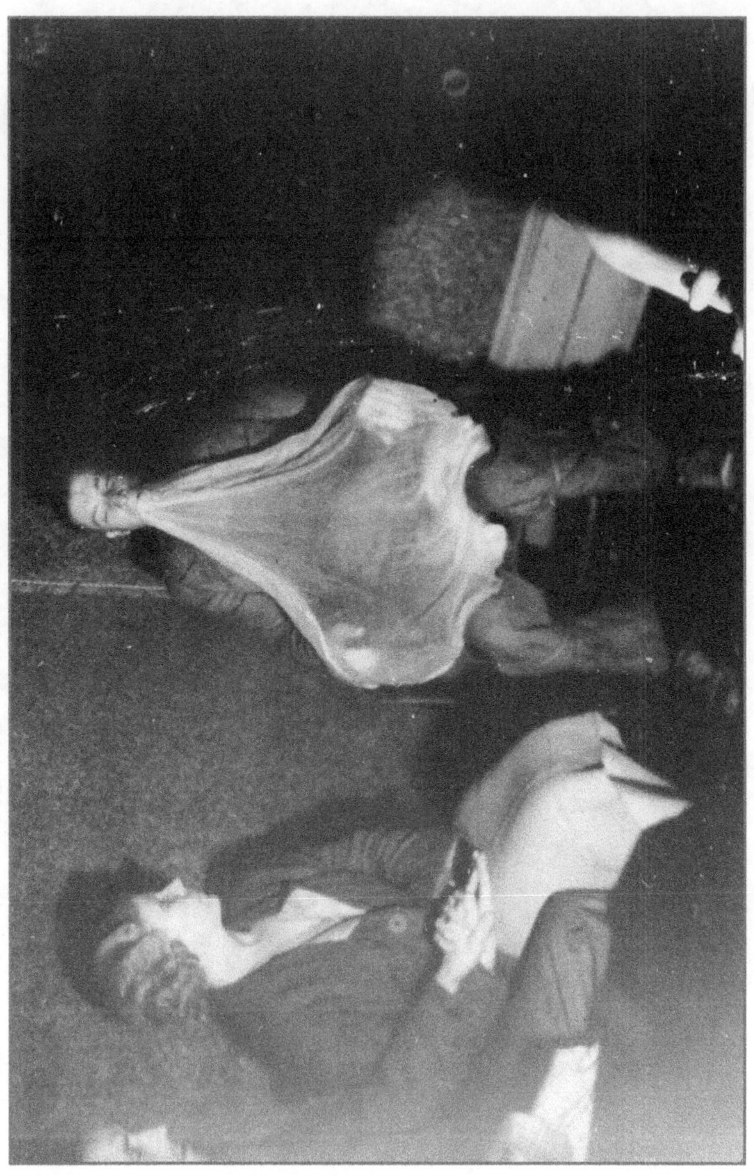

In this photograph the extremely fine ectoplasm is shown flowing over the medium's hands before lying in folds on his knee.

Note the fine bunched folds of ectoplasm issuing from the solar plexus of the medium's body. Ectoplasm may externalise from any orifice of the body. Though not obvious to us, the solar plexus is one.

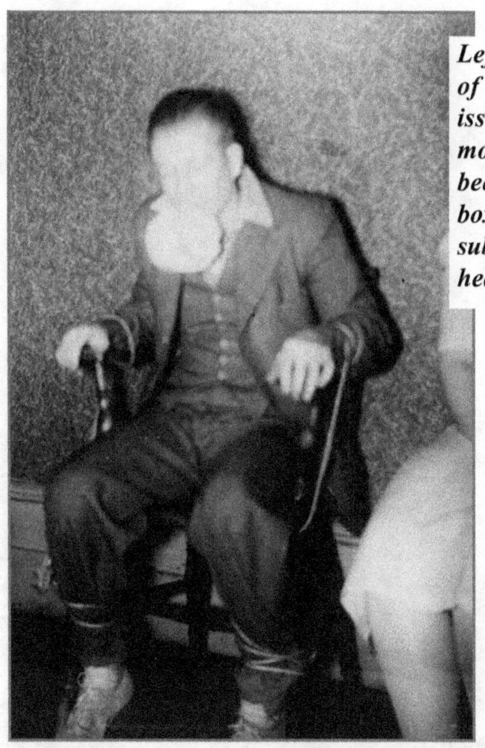

Left: A similar formation of bunched ectoplasm issues from the medium's mouth. This may have been to produce a voice box or the flow of the fine substance draped above his head as shown below.

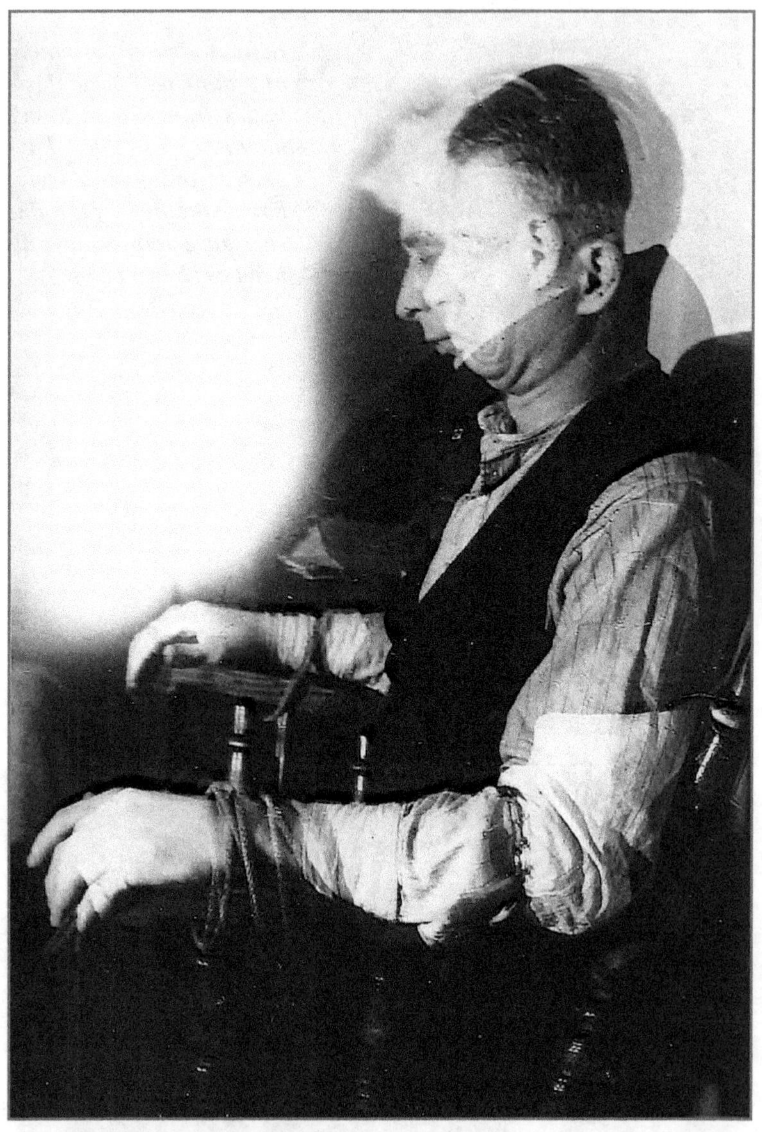

Infra-red photo taken by Mr W. Clayton with the object of elucidating the removal of the medium's jacket. The result appears at first sight to be a double exposure. The Guide, however, told them that the left face in not really like Webber.

(Originally published in'The Mediumship of Jack Webber')

One of the photographs (Plate 8 in *The Mediumship of Jack Webber*) taken by Mr W. Clayton was with the object of elucidating the removal of the medium's jacket. The result appears at first sight to be a double exposure (reproduced opposite). The Guide, however, has told them that the left face in not really like Webber. The hair in front is differently arranged, while the chin, so far as it is visible above the jacket collar, is prominent, whereas Webber's is noticeably receding. The profile as a whole is not the same. The natural conclusion is that the first exposure took place previously and is a portrait of someone else, However, the jacket which is around the left figure has the same badge that Webber always wears, and what has happened to the arms and the rest of the figure? Another questionable feature is the chair. It looks rather as though the far figure is sitting on a different chair. If so, the body difficulty crops up again while the hands contradict this theory. If the left hand is closely observed, it will be seen that it is either double or there are six fingers of which two are bent down, while there is something very odd about the little finger. Altogether apart from Mr Edwards' evidence it seems that there is internal evidence of the genuineness of the photograph and it therefore does show, beyond comprehension, how the coat is removed.

B. Abdy Collins was able to bear witness to two of the most striking phenomena ever performed in séances he attended. Once with Bernard Gray of the *Sunday Pictorial* a piece of plywood 12 inches x 9 inches, made phosphorescent on one side, floated light side up in the air close beside Gray. A mist appeared on it and this took shape as a perfectly formed human head and neck, smaller than life size but alive, with eyelids, lips etc., all moving naturally. Eventually it addressed him and gave him a name which was evidential to him.

The second feature was the removal of Webber's jacket. He was tied securely into the chair, his jacket was fastened in front with cotton thread, two people either side of him held both of his hands before the light was turned off and until after it was turned on again. During that short period of darkness Webber's jacket was removed and dropped on to the floor in front of him, passing not only through his body and the ropes but also felt by the sitters holding his hands.

On page 62 Harry Edwards refers in a report of a sitting for 'The Link Association of Home Circles' to Mrs Noah Zerdin 'lacing Webber into his jacket', and in *The Mediumship of Jack Webber*, Colin Evans, the medium, also writes of the stitching of the jacket:

> "Before he was tied in the chair, his coat was stitched all down the front so that it was an absolutely tight fit that could not possibly be taken off or put on again, even if his arms had been free, without undoing the stitching. I examined the stitching and noted "trappy" ways it was caught and twisted round certain buttons that would have "given away" any interference made by resewing. After the seance, it took some minutes to cut away this stitching with scissors."

While examining the original photographs recently it was found that the stitching had been caught on camera in a couple of photographs taken of the removal of the jacket, which we have been able to enlarge. *(original shown below)*

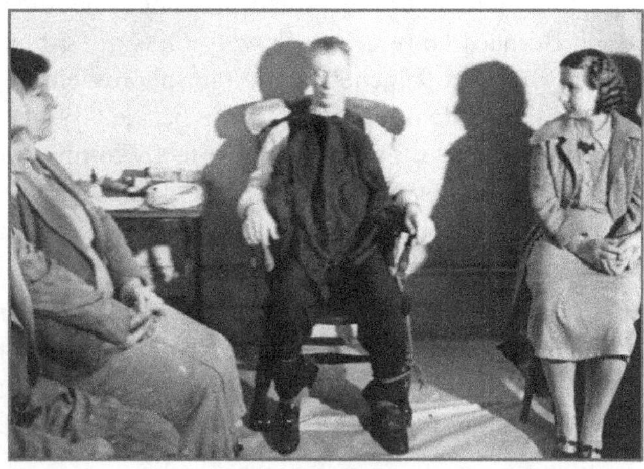

In this enlargement of the photograph opposite you can observe a sitter has closely stitched the front of the jacket and this stitching is still in place when the jacket has been removed. Is that a closed safety pin at the bottom buttonhole?

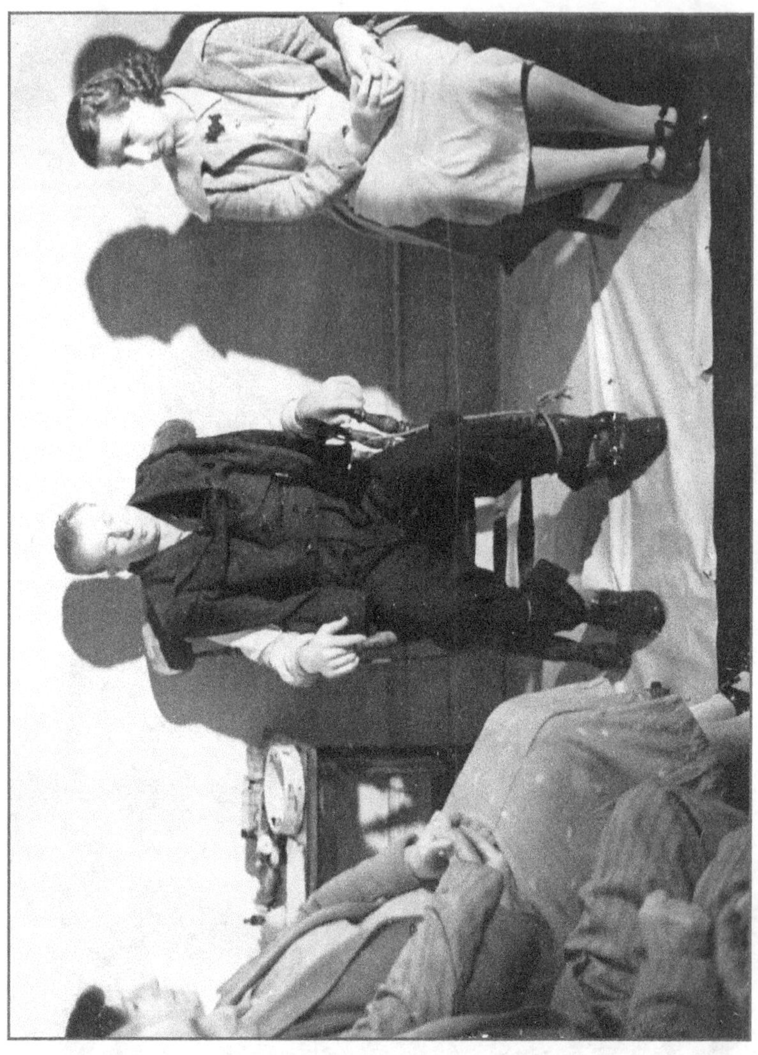

In this previously unpublished photograph, the jacket is only partly removed from the medium's body. The sleeves are off the arms but the main part of the jacket is rumpled up the medium's torso. The back appears to be riding up around his shoulders as in McCullough's photograph on page 102 .

On close examination the stitching is seen in a diagonal line across his chest. (enlargement from photograph opposite.)

One incident Mr Collins claimed to have seen in a description of a séance at a private house at which Mr Evans (my Grampa) Jack's father-in-law, was said to have switched the light on by mistake and Jack was discovered standing up, his leg still tied to the chair, his arms free, with a trumpet held to his mouth. Jack, who bled copiously at the nose following this, continued the sitting and appeared afterwards to be unconscious of what had happened. This, it would seem, was an inexplicable, isolated incident not unlike that which happened to Colin Fry during a séance he was holding for the Noah's Ark Society when he was found out of his binds and holding a trumpet after the lights were accidently switched on.[4] Knowing what Jack was like my Grampa begged those present not to mention anything to Jack as he knew he would never sit again.

By the end of his short time in London Jack had sat in around 400 seances, without public exposure. If control of the lights was of such vital importance, then it is curious that he travelled alone so often and allowed strangers to be in control of the light. Jack Webber was ready to agree to pretty much any test such was his trust in his Spirit team. Invariably it was Mr Edwards who would be the one to object and put a stop to new tests until they had been talked over within the confines of the home circle.

---

4. The Noah's Ark séance took place at Scole, Norfolk on 18th October 1992.

Chapter Eight

In the Midst of Life We are in Death

The new year started well with séances for the International Institute of Psychic Investigation – as documented in the previous chapter and as Addenda in Harry Edward's book, but Jack developed influenza during February and passed a few weeks later. His life cut short with an untimely passing on March 9th 1940 at the age of 32 years and 10 months.

There are several versions, by various authors, giving details of Jack's health condition in the days leading up to his passing. One version in Paul Miller's book, *Born to Heal*, the story of Harry Edwards from the mid 1950s, is taken from Harry Edwards' own book, *Science of Spirit Healing* (1943), and another briefer version is recalled by Harry Edwards in his own later book, *Spirit Healing* from 1960.

There is also an account which is included in my Grandmother, Nellie Evans' letter, from the late 1940s which she entitled "Family Saga of Psychic Gifts" some of which is already included in this book, detailing Jack's development and early years of his mediumship. Nellie writes;

"After living in Balham for a year, war had broken out, but Jack still carried on with his work, travelling long distances under great difficulties. He was taken ill with influenza but before he had time to properly recover, he undertook an engagement up north. On his return journey he travelled by train and when he entered the carriage it was already occupied by a soldier, who Jack believed was asleep. It soon became apparent to Jack that the soldier was quite ill. He leaned over the soldier to take his hand, to give him healing, and as he did so, the breath and germs from the soldier rose up into Jack's face. When he eventually arrived home from his eventful journey he retired to his bed, but the next morning, after returning home from a short walk, he collapsed and was made to return to his bed once more. He kept repeating that he could still smell the soldier's breath.

We called out the local doctor who said that it was still the influenza that Jack was suffering from, but as the day progressed, he steadily became worse. We called on my daughter, Winifred Rooke (a trance healer – working with Harry Edwards for the Balham Psychical Research Society) to attend to him. Her healing guide, *Bulzar,* came through and examined Jack and broke the news to us that he was suffering from spinal meningitis. The next day, when the doctor called around again, I asked him if he thought it could be spinal meningitis, he gave me a strange look but then said he would send for an ambulance. Jack was taken to hospital, where it was apparent that many soldiers lay dying from the same complaint as he. Jack Webber passed into Spirit on 9th March 1940."

The above is a very matter of fact version from an unlettered woman who put pen to paper shortly after the end of World War 2 to provide herself and her future family with a historical record of her family's involvement in the Spiritualist movement, and in particular to record the special gifts of her son-in-law and other gifted members of her family.

What others have said within their books, in recalling events which may or may not have played out exactly as they describe, is left up to the reader to decide. For me, my Gran's words are the ones I have known all my life and are the ones I will continue to live by.

Jack relaxing before going to a private séance

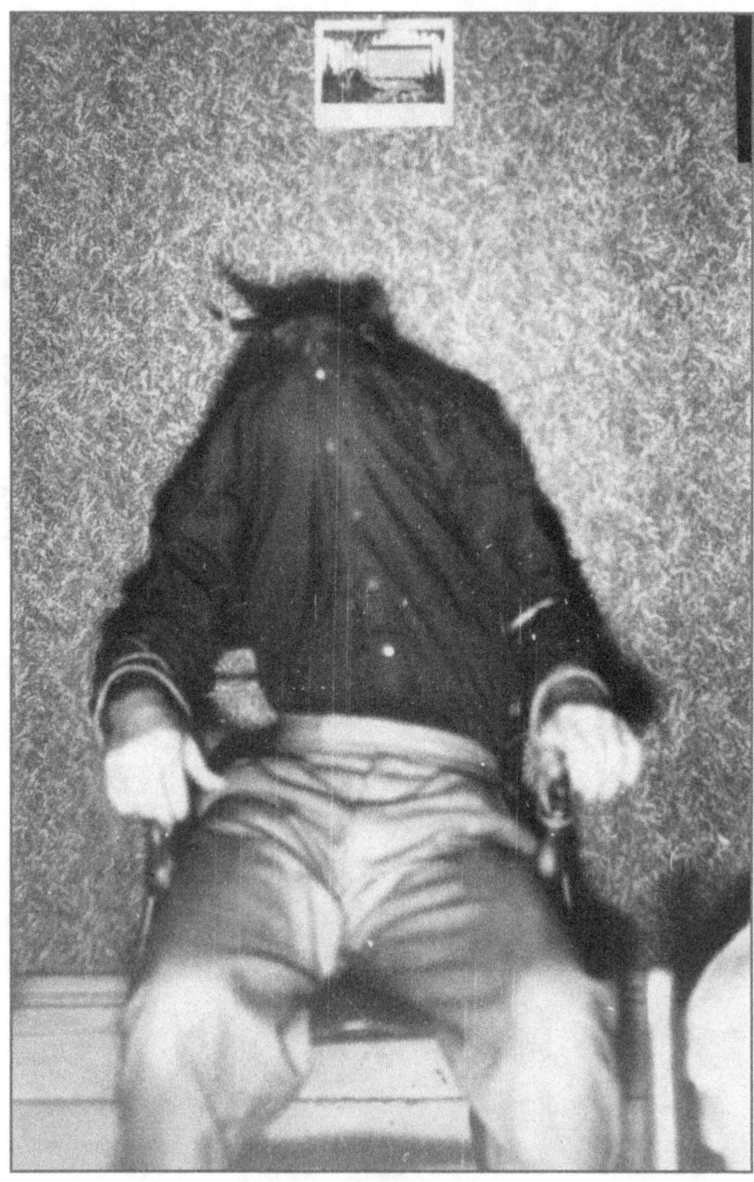

On this unusual occasion, having removed the medium's jacket, they attempted to remove his shirt. As there are no records we do not know if it was sucessful (previously unpublished).

Chapter Nine

"Post Mortem"

There was and has been speculation since the time of his passing that Jack had become a wealthy man. The simple truth behind these speculations is that that he had not become and was not wealthy. He may well have been considered as not too badly off by the standards of the day but it wasn't truly the case when one has to take into consideration that he had a wife and young family to support, as well as his in-laws who shared the same house as him during that period.

The average price a person would pay to sit in a séance with Jack Webber in February 1940 was seven shillings and sixpence (7/6d) this equates to around £16.00 (as already quoted) per head in today's money. At that time, just prior to his passing, Jack received, on average, an income of around £10-£12 per week which equates to around £530 to £630 per week in today's money. This would be accrued through potentially putting himself at risk 3-4 times a week, in subjecting himself to taxing séance conditions, whether with one or two private sitters taking part in his home development circles in Balham or travelling, often on his own, to privately arranged circles at private homes or Spiritualist Churches around the country.

Jack has been accused of being a bit of a gambler and prone to wasting his money particularly at the Penny Arcade on Balham High Street and I don't seek to defend Jack in this matter because it's true! He did like to wander down to the High Street, sometimes with Harry Edwards for company, to spend an afternoon on the slots. His especial favourite for whiling the time away was the 'Crane machine'. Nowadays this type of machine is filled with fluffy toys which one must try and extricate with a dodgy claw grabber. Back then they were filled with more elaborate items such as lighters, pens, watches, cigarettes and note cases etc. These items, among others which Jack desired, seemed to be magically lifted by the mechanical claw and dropped into the dispenser. His winning streak reached such a pitch that the proprietor of the amusement arcade banned the pair of them from playing these machines. This information was relayed to me fairly recently through an exchange of letters I had with Harry's youngest daughter, Felicity Medland, and is also recorded in a biography on the life of Harry Edwards by Ramus (Ray) Branch.

When I originally heard the story of Jack's fondness for gambling, I was actually reluctant to accept the idea that he could possibly have squandered his money in this manner. Naturally, one would hope that he would not have done this had he known that his life was to be cut short and that his family would be left penniless.

However, I have recently heard a recording which exactly confirms this to be the case. The medium through whom Jack spoke on that occasion is a lady called Sandy Sinclair. I've had the pleasure of meeting and sitting with Sandy on several occasions. On this occasion, however, Jack came through to speak with renowned Scottish medium, Mary Armor, who was to be presenting a talk on Jack's mediumship at a Noah's Ark Society seminar at Burton on Trent (3rd May 1997), the day following her sitting with Sandy.

Jack told her that he was pleased she was to give a talk about him and that he would be there with her. He also added that his boots got a bit too big for him, that he thought it was all him, when in fact it was those working through him who should have received the credit for the phenomena and communication produced. He also told Mary that he liked to gamble, that he loved to go down the Arcade and put his money in the slots, also adding that his wife Rhoda didn't like it and that she would give him a clip around the lughole if ever she found out. It transpired that he did indeed leave his wife Rhoda and their two sons penniless when he passed.

Jack and Rhoda's two boys. Denzil aged eight and George aged six. (From original print by permission of George Webber.)

Jack's immediate family came up from Wales, it is alleged, hoping to discover some riches that he had left behind him. This was clearly not the case, as on 14th March 1940, at Streatham Cemetery, following an emotional and very well attended funeral service, Jack Webber's body was interred in a public multiple grave, known as a Pauper's Grave, which he shared with at least seven other bodies. This wasn't, however, to be his final resting place!

His body was, at some point, with no official records to corroborate this, exhumed and sent for cremation. This information was provided to me by Jack's younger son, George who emigrated to Canada with his mother and her new partner, a Canadian soldier, in September 1946 on one of the SS Queen Mary repatriation trips. There he and his brother grew up, eventually married and had families of their own. George, now around 85 years of age, has little memory of his father or the hardships that followed his passing but he and his extended family are happy to be living in Canada and he is always delighted to hear any information that comes to light about his father.

George and Mary Webber in Canada 2019

Following the receipt of this information I approached the records department for Streatham Cemetery and discovered that Jack's final resting place is Area 475, Plot 12, the position in the cemetery where his ashes are indeed buried.

Will I ever visit this place, probably not! I have spoken with Uncle Jack on a number of occasions through the trance mediumship of various members of my family. He is not in the ground – he has indeed slipped from earth to air, and found his waiting loved ones there.

Jack's passing was so unexpected that an advert had been placed with *Psychic News,* appearing just five days before his death, for demonstrations etc at 11 Childerbert Road.

BALHAM PSYCHIC RESEARCH SOCIETY

11, Childebert Road, Balham, S.W.17.

JACK WEBBER

Demonstrations include Direct Voice, Levitations, Materialisations and other forms of physical phenomena.

Churches and Circles visited. Private group sittings held, afternoons and evenings (7/6).

Mrs. W. ROOK

Trance Speaker, Clairvoyant, etc., has open dates for engagements—also for private readings. Development Classes now being formed.

All letters and applications for Spiritual Healing to Harry Edwards.

Psychic News advertisement in early March 1940

When Jack passed in March 1940, prior to the publication of Harry Edwards' book of Jack's mediumship, there was in place a gentleman's agreement between them which said they would each take an equal share of any profits created from the sale of the book. Although a very successful book with 3,500 copies sold during the first three months following publication, and countless further copies in the years that followed, not one penny of the royalties found their way back to Jack's wife,

Rhoda, or their two sons. Harry even borrowed the necessary money from the Jack Webber Memorial Fund to fund the publication of 'their' book.

In January 2019 I received a letter from Felicity Medland, Harry Edward's 95-year-old daughter, in reply to a letter I had written to her. She wrote:

"The agreement you mention between Jack and Dad over the Royalties of the book, became null and void when Jack died." She continued "As the author and bearer of the expenses of publishing the book, what Dad did with the royalties was up to him." She also said "I do agree, as you have written, that he could and should have done more to help Rhoda and her family."

As previously mentioned, the funds to publish the book were not actually borne directly by Harry Edwards. He borrowed the money, non-consensually, from the memorial fund set up to help Jack's family. The £80.00, plus a further £20.00, that were taken from the fund to cover publication costs for his book were eventually repaid to the fund with the profits made from the first ninety books sold. Records also show that the costs for advertising, postage and packaging were also taken from the memorial fund as and when required. It is understandable why for the many decades that followed the Webber and Evans family members fell out with Harry for what they construed to be an underhanded and greedy act.

A copy of payments under the agreement taken from Harry Edwards accounts book/records is opposite. This confirms the agreement to have still been in force as of November 1941 but which was not followed up with further Royalty payments to the family in any shape or form.

INCOME.

By total receipts including donations and monies for sale of Records up to November I94I	£246- 2- 2
By receipts for Gramophone records and 9/6d donations to March Ioth, I94I	6-I2- 0
By receipt for sales of books	80- 3-I0
	£332-I8 -0

EXPENDITURE

By payments to Mrs. Webber	£75-I4- 2	
By expenditure payments	I35- 2-II	
	£2I0-I7- I	2I0-I7- I
		£ I22- 0-II

Balance in hand £I22-0-II

Notes.--The payments to Mrs. Webber are straitforward.
Expenditure. The £80 used to purchase books (a condition of publication) has been repaid into bank from book receipts. A verbal Agreement was made between Jack Webber and H.J. Edwards to divide equally profits. The latter holds this to be good for the Fund, so that 50% of the profits will be paid into fund asx and when received.
Mr. Edwards also advanced £20 purchase of books,(publishers condition(£I00 in all)the £80 was the first obligation, and the £20 is now in course of repayment. The next charge against income from the books will be the paying into the fund of the amount of £I6-0-6 advertising charges (this amount includes the cost of advertising records as well. This latter sum is assumed secured by books on hand and royalties due. Postages include all payments of appeals and notices for books besides postages for receipts of donations and letters, as well as on records and books. The latter(records and books) have be previously paid by purchasers but is not shown separately. All printed matter for appeals and book notices, receipts, labels and all other such matter, in cluding all stationery, and other such goods have been provided by H. Edwards without charge to the fund

The Memorial Fund, set up and overseen by Harry Edwards, was indeed a blessing for Jack's young family until it finally lapsed after eighteen months. The funding came by way of a huge outpouring from the Spiritualist community, with donations coming in from dozens of Churches, those famous in the Spiritualist community, the public, and by way of events organized to raise money for the fund.

Also added to the fund were profits from the sales of the Decca 78rpm Record of Jack's Guide, *Reuben*, singing. This was quite a minimal amount but still a welcome addition to the pot. Some of the first people recorded – and some of them on more than one occasion – in contributing, to the fund were: Mr Oaten of *The Two Worlds*, Mr Barbanell of *Psychic News,* Mr Leslie Flint, 31 Sydney Grove, Hendon, Mr Harold Sharp and Circle, 'The Link' public 'Voice' séance with Ronald Strong....

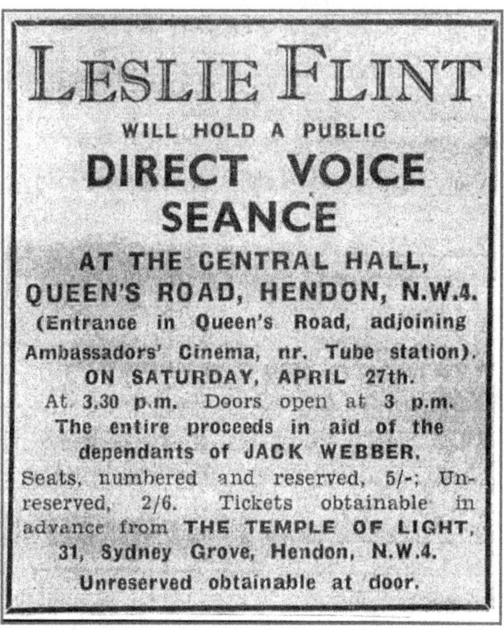

Advert in 'Psychic News' for a Leslie Fint Demonstration for Jack's family

...along with several donations from America, Canada and Germany, and from many who just signed their accompanying letter; from a Friend or Anon.

Here is a small selection of those letters taken from amongst the hundreds received at 11 Childebert Street, H.Q. for Balham Psychic Research Society, under the Leadership of Harry Edwards, following the passing of John Boaden Webber.

REGISTERED BY THE JOINT COUNCIL OF QUALIFIED OPTICIANS FOR SIGHT TESTING AND OPTICAL TREATMENT UNDER THE NATIONAL HEALTH INSURANCE ACTS.

Horace A. Jones

M.P.S., F.S.M.C., F.I.O.

Qualified Chemist & Optician.

170, Beech Avenue,

Northampton.

Photographic work a speciality.

B.P.R.S (Pres)

7/4/41.

Dear Sir

Please send me the Gramophone record of the Spirit voice of Reuben singing "Lead Kindly Light" + There's a Land".

Herewith P.O. for 6/6.

"Good Luck" under very trying conditions.

Yours Sincerely.

H.A. Jones.

A Letter from Northampton requesting a copy of the Gramophone Record of "Reuben" singing.

73. Heywood Street
Alexandra Park
Manchester 16
July 9/40

Dear Mr Edwards
- Enclosed please find Postal
Order for 13/-
And shall be glad if You will kindly
forward at Your earliest convenience
The Book entitled
"The Mediumship of Jack Webber"

Yours Faithfully
(Miss) L. Eastwood
Hon Secretary
of the South Manchester National
Spiritualist Church Princess Hall
3 Princess Road Moss Side
Manchester

Above: A Letter from the secretary of the South Manchester National Spiritualist Church requesting a book.

Facing page top: A donation via 'Psychic News' from a regular reader in Bideford.

Facing page below: A letter from Yorkshire requesting a book and donating the balance to the Memorial Fund.

THE SPIRITUALIST NEWSPAPER WITH THE WORLD'S LARGEST CIRCULATION.

Psychic News.

TELEPHONE: HOLBORN 2914/5.
TELEGRAMS: PSYCHICS, WESTCENT, LONDON.

144, HIGH HOLBORN.
(1 MINUTE FROM HOLBORN TUBE STATION.)
LONDON, W.C.1.

PROPRIETORS: PSYCHIC PRESS LTD.
DIRECTORS: J. ARTHUR FINDLAY. MAURICE BARBANELL.

EVERY THURSDAY.

21st October, 1940.

Dear Mr. Edwards,

re: JACK WEBBER MEMORIAL FUND

I am enclosing 2/6d towards the above from one of our readers. Will you send him a receipt? His name and address are E. S. Jenkins, Myrtle Cottage, Westleigh, Bideford, North Devon.

Yours truly,
PSYCHIC PRESS LTD.
J. N[illegible]
Secretary

Harry Edwards, Esq.,

13, Belmont Avenue
South Bank
Yorks.
14 Aug. 1940.

Harry Edwards, Esq.
11 Childebert Road,
London. S.W.17.

Dear Sir,

Will you please send me "The Mediumship of Jack Webber".

Enclosed is £1 to pay for same, and will you please apply the balance to the Memorial Fund.

Yours faithfully,
Jim Lackenby

Harry Edwards, a great orator as well as, in later years, a prolific author, also took it upon himself to give his services through the demonstration of Film Slides and lecture on Jack's mediumship. This he gave freely to all churches in the Greater London area, but only if the proceeds may be devoted to the Memorial Fund. There were several emotional appeals published in the various Spiritualist papers of the time from the hand of Harry Edwards. One such read:

> "Dear Friend, In sending you this appeal, may I add a personal word, in the hope that we may receive your sympathetic co-operation. During the short time Jack Webber was with us (16 months) we endeavoured to safeguard the mediumship by strictly limiting the number of times he sat each week. On no occasion was this ever exceeded. This limitation added to the reasons stated in the accompanying appeal dealing with the position of the family, which due to his generous commitments (not for himself) prevented the maturing of plans that had been made for their future security. I feel that it is only fair to all who are being approached to assist the Memorial Fund to make this clear, for it may well and justifiably be in the minds of friends that his fees should have been able to make some provision for the future.
>
> Having explained the position, I personally feel, that in view of Jack Webber's service to the movement and the fact that he never refused to serve a Church or any person on account of means, that this is an occasion when our movement as a whole should stand by those left behind. If the position could be explained to your people, I am sure they would, out of the goodness of the heart, respond to a special or retiring collection or by any other means that you may consider suitable. Bound as we all are by the common ideals of our faith – to help one another – I do not hesitate to appeal to you for your help for so worthy a cause and feel that this appeal will not be sent to you in vain."
>
> Yours truly, Harry Edwards

A full reproduction of the original appeal accompanied this letter.

BALHAM PSYCHIC RESEARCH SOCIETY

(incorporating The Fellowship of Spiritual Service)

SPIRITUAL HEALING AND PSYCHIC DEVELOPMENT CENTRE

Leader, HARRY EDWARDS

11, CHILDEBERT ROAD, BALHAM, LONDON, S.W.17.

Telephone STReatham 0323

HARRY EDWARDS
Spiritual Healing
Addresses Clairvoyance
Film Slide Exhibition
with address on the
Mediumship late Mr. Jack Webber

Mrs. WINIFRED ROOKE
Spiritual Healing
Trance Addresses
Clairvoyance and
Psychometry
Private Readings

EDDIE DAVIES
Transfiguration
Spiritual Healing Tuesday evenings
7 p.m. or by appointment
Developing Circles

JACK WEBBER MEMORIAL FUND

THE MEDIUM.

The sudden passing of Jack Webber has proved a great shock to his many friends in the spiritualist movement and the loss of his mediumship will be greatly missed. His quiet unassuming friendly nature and his entire lack of egotism concerning his gifts, endeared him to all he came in contact with.

During his work no applicant or mourner was ever denied an opportunity of obtaining knowledge or comfort on account of means. On most occasions a number of free seats were given at his home seances. For Parties for Spirit Children he always gave his services voluntary, as well as to home circles who needed advice and help from his Guides.

To spread the truth of survival Jack co-operated willingly with the Press and sat several times for them without monetary reward.

In the task of furthering human knowledge of the powers of the spirit people and to obtain photographic evidence of the super-normal he never failed to place himself at our disposal and at the service of his Guides. A complete selection of these photographs with a narrative of the records is about to be published and will give to the world a permanent record of the lessons to be learned from his mediumship.

In his private life he maintained other members of the family, his mother and father, as well as his own family. Generous to a fault he was ever ready to give assistance to a friend in distress.

During the past eighteen months that this young medium was working, he redeemed past liabilities and his commitments were so heavy that he was unable to provide in time for the future.

THE NEED.

His generous and care-free nature has left his wife and two young sons in sore need. They are without any means for the moment or any source of income for the future.

When Jack Webber's services to our movement are remembered, the consolation and help given to so many in need, the many seances given to help Church funds, etc., it is confidently hoped that many will feel it a privilege and a duty to come to the aid of his family.

MEMORIAL FUND

A memorial fund has therefore been opened and the undersigned have formed themselves into a honorary committee of management.

It is hoped that through the generosity of the movement, that not only may the immediate dread of destitution be removed but that some practical form of appreciation of his work may be established, if only to provide facilities for the education of his two young sons, aged 7 and 9.

Individual donations are asked for, and it is hoped that not only those Churches who have received benefit from the mediumship, but all others will join in a united effort to assist this appeal by collections or other means.

SUGGESTION.

Mr. Harry Edwards is willing to give the demonstration of Film Slides and lecture on the mediumship, freely, to all churches in the Greater London area, if the proceeds may be devoted to the Memorial Fund. This exhibition and lecture provides the photographic evidence of survival and has of late been increasingly used for Sunday services as well as on weekdays.

There also remain a number (under 50) of the gramophone recording of Jack Webber's control Rueben singing "Lead Kindly Light" and "There's a Land" which can be supplied so long as they last. As all the profits will be devoted to the Fund, applicants for these are asked to be as generous as possible.

It may be mentioned that at no time has the above Society or anyone connected with it ever profited financially from the mediumship—all services having been voluntary given.

All donations will be gratefully acknowledged individually and reports will be published in the Psychic Press.

We the undersigned having been informed of the distress in which the family has been unfortunatly left, earnestly appeal to his many friends in the movement to assist in removing the dread of the future from the family of one who served our Cause so faithfully and well

Signed Harry Edwards, *Chairman.*
Stanley Croft
Jack McCulloch
Gladys Layton

In spite of all that has gone before I personally carry no malice towards Mr Edwards, for had it not been for his endeavours in befriending and sponsoring Jack then there is much that may not have been achieved, or come to fruition. Had it not been for his intervention there may not have been a book published extolling Jack's amazing mediumship.

There may not have been eighteen months of exceptional London séances with the wonderful Physical Phenomena that developed because of it. There may not have been such an abundance of national newspaper articles or indeed reports published within the annals of our historical *Psychic News* and *The Two Worlds* spiritual publications. There may not have been the funds available to help establish Burrows Lea in 1946 as the Harry Edwards Healing Sanctuary, now in its seventy-third year, as the most successful, worldwide centre for Spiritual Healing.

There is much to be grateful for, and I think it is fair to say that these two men were destined to meet and be brought together for the good of our movement and perhaps for the betterment of all who ever crossed their paths.

Appendix One

Winifred Rooke

Winifred Rooke was the sister-in-law of Jack Webber. She worked alongside him and Harry Edwards as leaders of the Balham Psychic Research Society.

She also had played an instrumental part in bringing Jack into the movement some twelve or more years earlier, as she was the young physical medium in whose home circle Jack began to sit so that he could spend more time with his girlfriend Rhoda, Winifred's sister.

In 1933 she married Harry Rooke in Barnstable, Devon. Her sceptical partner had been part of the Plymouth Brethren Society but he eventually, through his research, discovered the truth and beauty of Spiritualism. In early 1940, Harry was to be called away into the Army, he was stationed in Aldershot (home of the British Army) and on that basis Winifred decided, for the sake of some familiar company, that she would also come to live with her family in Balham. She gave her services to many churches in and around the London area and also gave her services as a healer to the newly created Balham Psychic Research Society which had initially been started by Harry Edwards and Jack Webber.

As mentioned in the section relating to Jack's illness which led to his passing, it was Winifred's healing guide who was called upon to try and help Jack, following the doctor's diagnosis of his continued influenza. *Bulzar*, a North American Indian, working through Winifred who was in a deep trance state, diagnosed Jack's condition of spinal meningitis which eventually led to his hospitalisation and passing to spirit.

Winifred was quite a draw at Childebert Road healing sanctuary, as her work was considered to be of a very high standard. Only a few weeks following Jack's passing a newspaper reporter from the *Balham, Tooting, Mitcham News & Mercury* visited Mrs Rooke as a patient and experienced a remarkable evening at Balham.

This report was published Friday March 29th, 1940.

> "The other evening writes one of our reporters, I attended a faith healing meeting. I went a sceptic; I came away the most puzzled man in Christendom. I went with a nice theory. I came away with that theory upset. The theory was that fully 90% of illnesses owe their beginnings to a psychological state and that if that mental state can be remedied the illness would disappear. But I saw a man who had been deaf for twenty years hear the voice of the healer, through the medium. Even then the medium had difficulty in making him believe the evidence of his own ears. For twenty years that man had understood people only by lip reading yet now he heard words spoken from behind his back.
>
> In ordinary circumstances, when you see a doctor you tell him where the pain is, and he tells you what the trouble is. Mrs Rooke stood behind each patient and told her or him where the pain was!
>
> An objective report ...the faith healing meeting was at the home of Mr Harry Edwards, at 11 Childebert Road, Balham and was held under the auspices of the Balham Psychic Research Society. The medium was Mrs Winifred Rooke, who came to Balham from Plymouth seven weeks ago. Her guide or healer was *Bulzar*, a North American Indian. After attending the meeting, I neither recommend nor otherwise the efficacy of faith

healing. That is a responsibility too great for me to undertake. I can only report, objectively, what happened and let our readers come to their own conclusions. The first patient was a sufferer from shellshock during the great war. Since the end of the last war he has suffered from head and eye trouble and though he has attended hospitals and had his head X-rayed, no doctor has been able to diagnose the trouble or cure him. It is only since he has been receiving healing that he has secured relief. Five weeks ago, the healer, through Mrs Rooke, preformed an operation putting in their right places two bones at the base of the skull and from that time the patient has felt better. Before the operation, the patient told me, "A light would come in the centre of my forehead and I would lose consciousness. I had a light yesterday, that's why I came here tonight, but it wasn't as bad as it had been before."

The next patient was a new one, and I watched the medium, who was in a trance throughout, tell her what the trouble was. She told the patient she had had a nasty shock some time ago and this had upset the balance of her system. The patient remembered the shock and agreed that all the aches and pains the healer mentioned were true. The next was also a new patient and here again *Bulzar* was able to tell where the trouble was and to give healing rays and relief.

The fourth patient was the deaf man. Although he said he could not hear, the medium, by talking to him from behind his back was able to prove that he could hear. She told him that his trouble was that he could now hear but he had become so accustomed to lip-reading that his brain had to become used again to translating the sounds received through the ear. And to prove that he could hear, the medium walked further and further away, each time asking the man questions which he answered. To prove the medium's suggestion that he did indeed have difficulty in translating words, he said "I can hear you, but cannot distinguish the words!"

After two more patients were treated, each testifying to the improvement they had felt since receiving healing, it was my turn! I am normally a healthy person.

By that I mean that I occasionally suffer from some of the minor ills of the flesh. One of those ailments was a touch of catarrh, a hangover from a bad cold...could the medium of *Bulzar* spot this I wondered? The first question I was asked was: "What do you want of me?" but before I had time to answer, the medium went on "You have only a slight catarrh and occasionally you suffer from indigestion so that you cannot easily sleep at night." Both these facts were perfectly true and so was the fact, which the medium told me, that I occasionally suffered from rheumatism. "You also have a good appetite" she went on. Another perfectly true fact, since I can always eat four good meals a day, with a snack in between. "That probably accounts for your indigestion." She also told me "You also read a lot in artificial light." Another true fact but not one she could have told from the condition of my eyes, since I have exceptional good eyesight, having recently passed an eye test with flying colours. "There is nothing seriously wrong with you," I was told "but I will give you the healing rays, since you have a receptive mind." The medium placed her hands on my head, her fingers were vibrating, and I could feel a tingle down my spine. The nearest to humour during the whole evening, which otherwise was carried out in a reverent atmosphere was when she told me, with a smile, "You will now have a greater appetite than ever."

Mr Edwards, afterward, told me of some of the cases she had cured at Plymouth. One was a boy of seven, crippled since birth with infantile paralysis.

His leg was twisted round, and he could only crawl. But *Bulzar* performed two operations involving the breaking of bones in his leg. During those operations no anaesthetic was used; the boy was put into a sleeping trance state and felt no pain whatsoever. He is now cured. Another case was an old lady whose hands were so crippled and twisted with neuritis that she could not use them. Following progressive healing she now has perfect use of both hands. Other cases include several patients with tuberculosis and other with internal organ displacement, all cured following two or three treatment at the hands of Mrs Rooke and her guide *Bulzar*."

Mrs Winifred Rooke - Trance healer

Appendix Two

International Interest

Thanks to *Psychic News,* the knowledge of Jack's mediumship was spreading across the world. The cutting opposite was found in Harry Edwards' scrapbook.

The British army had a large presence in the Meerut District of Uttar-Pradesh in Northern India at the time, and presumably their families were there too. Someone must have subscribed to the *Psychic News* for this photograph from the front page of November 26th 1938 was published in "The "PARALOKA" Meerut" (Volume 6 No 5).

The Hindi word 'Paraloka' translates as 'Heaven' or 'The Other World' but as to what else is written we cannot say. Maybe just what is printed below it in English. And did the article follow it ? We shall never know.

Regd. No. A. 2394.

Volume 6 *No. 5*

The "PARALOKA" Meerut.

"परलोक"

❀ मेरठ ❀

यह चित्र लन्दन में गत नवम्बर १६३८ में रात्रि में होते हुवे एक प्रयोग के समय लिया गया था। माध्यम बीच में बैठा है उसके हाथ और पैर कुर्सी से रस्सियों द्वारा बंधे हुवे हैं उसके मुंह और वक्षस्थल से कुछ सफेद पदार्थ निकल रहा है उसके सिर पर दो तुरियां हैं जिन में से परलोकगत आत्माओं का शब्द सुनाई देता है। विशेष परिचय पृष्ठ ११३ पर देखें।

[The Picture was taken for "Psychic News" by Lean Isaacs. It is the copyright of the Fellowship of Spiritual Service Balham, where the seance was held.]

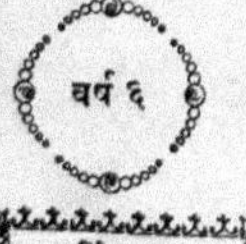

जनवरी १६३६

वार्षिक मूल्य
२॥)

सम्पादकः— श्री केदारनाथ शर्मा
श्री जी० वी० साठे

एक प्रति
।)

www.ingramcontent.com/pod-product-compliance
Lightning Source LLC
LaVergne TN
LVHW051131080426
835510LV00018B/2356

* 9 7 8 1 9 0 8 4 2 1 3 6 4 *